CATHAR COUNTRY

An independent holiday guide
to
CARCASSONNE

and the *département*
of
AUDE

Trevor Park

© 2009 Trevor Park   ISBN 978-0-9508325-3-1
St Bega Publications, St Bees, Cumbria CA27 0AF
Production by Country Books

Welcome to Carcassonne and the *département* of Aude

When you come, you will quickly discover what an area of outstanding natural beauty Aude is and what a wealth of history it has for you to explore and enjoy. The county town of Carcassonne has just over 47,000 inhabitants but it is reckoned to be second only to Paris in the number of visitors it attracts. Over two million people come here each year and most of them come in the summer. At times it can get very crowded in the *Cité* which is the top attraction. With the additional publicity it was given by Kate Mosse's best selling novels *Labyrinth* and *Sepulchre* the number of visitors from the UK has risen markedly – and thanks to the low-cost airline Ryanair which flies 370,000 passengers a year from Cork, Dublin, Shannon, the East Midlands, Liverpool and Stansted. Their new route from Edinburgh which opens in 2009 is expected to bring a further 40,000 visitors.

This independent guidebook offers a wealth of choice of places to see and things to do for people of all ages and tastes. It is divided into short, easy-to-manage sections arranged thematically for ease of reference. It will help your advance planning in a big way whilst being light enough not to weigh down your luggage. It is aimed both at the novice and the connoisseur of this region – offering something for everyone. My family has been coming to this area for many years and we have had a home near Carcassonne for the past eight. We have visited all the tourist sites described in this guide, some of them many times, so I can recommend them with confidence. I have given details of their websites where these exist so that you can find out more about the particular places or activities which are of special interest to you – it also allows you to check out opening times and admission charges in the month you will be visiting, and to get the latest information about what's on when you will be here. The centre page is a map of the *département* published by the Aude Tourist Board and I have provided a grid reference on this map for every site described in the book.

One consequence of the decline in the local wine industry is that much more attention is now being given to tourism. Even small villages are now laying on cultural events and entertainment which will be of interest to visitors and they are publicising these attractions more effectively. It is worth calling in at the village tourist information offices to find out what is going on locally whilst you are down here. If you can come in the spring or later in the autumn when it is still warm and sunny, you will find the *Cité* and the beaches far less crowded.

There is every likelihood that you will enjoy your visit so much that you will want to return and maybe even explore the possibility of relocating here. For those tempted to do this, I have included some basic information about house hunting and the practicalities of living here.

Bonnes vacances! Enjoy your holiday.   **Trevor Park**

Contents

Acknowledgements: Thanks to the Aude Tourist Board for permission to use the map on pages 30-31 and to the Carcassonne Tourist Board for permission to use the maps on pages 5 and 6. Thanks also to Alan Reynolds for the 8 sketch maps on pages 48-52, to the *OT Aude-en-Pyrénées* for the Aude river picture on page 16 and to Tim Mitchley for pictures of the *Cité* and of the castles. And lastly to Sunniva Park and others for their critical reading of the text.

Front cover illustrations: the *Cité* seen from the south in winter, and at the top of the page: the *Canal du Midi* at Le Somail, the beach at Narbonne Plage, market day in the lower city of Carcassonne, and Queribus Castle.
Back cover illustrations: the map of the *Cité* displayed outside the Count's castle.

All information was correct when this Guide was printed but opening times and admission fees etc may have changed since then. Do check the websites for the latest information. The author would welcome your comments and suggestions for amendments and additions in the next edition; please mail them to tpcarcassonne@btinternet.com Thank you.

Correction!
p.18 *La Cité des Oiseaux*
has closed permanently.

2012 Amendments
Updated information at
www.stbegabooks.com

Carcassonne – *La Cité*

A tingle of excited anticipation may well be your immediate reaction on first seeing the *Cité*. For this is the best restored medieval walled city in Europe. UNESCO designated it a World Heritage Site in 1997.

Standing high above the River Aude and with its twin concentric walls and 52 towers, its drawbridges and inner castle, it is the realisation of every child's dream of what a fortified city looks like. When you walk along its crowded, narrow streets or sit by the moat outside the *Château Comtal*, it's not hard to imagine yourself back in the 13th century. Come in July or August and you can watch actors dressed as medieval knights jousting in the *lices*, the grassy area between the outer and inner walls. And there are plenty of shops where plastic or wooden swords and shields can be bought, and space enough in the *lices* or along the ramparts where children (and adults) can live out their fantasy of being a knight, defending the city against the northern invaders in 1209. For a fortnight in mid-August there is a medieval festival at which part of the history of the city is re-enacted, and there is plenty of street entertainment with jugglers, and fire-eaters and musicians. If you are here on Bastille Day, July 14th, you can watch *L'embrasement de la Cité*, a spectacular firework display.

Despite not starting until 22.30 and lasting just half an hour, vast crowds of spectators come to see it. It is as though the entire *Cité* were ablaze – pictured top right next page.

There has been a fortified settlement here since the 6th century BC. It was held first by the Gauls, then by the Romans, followed by the Visigoths, Saracens and Franks. Its golden age was from 1089-1209 when the Trencavels, who were also Viscounts of Beziers and Nimes, were its rulers. Like many other tolerant, southern noble families they allowed Jews and adherents of the Cathar faith to live in their cities. The Cathars or *Bon Hommes* who saw themselves as the true heirs of Christ posed a serious challenge to the dominant and decadent Roman Catholic Church. In 1208 following the killing of a Papal Legate, Pope Innocent III called for a crusade against these heretics. At this time the region in the deep south was not part of France and it was an army of northern knights who waged war with the blessing not just of the Pope but also of the French King who saw it as an opportunity to extend the borders of his kingdom. The *Cité* fell to the crusaders after a short siege in the summer of 1209 and on the death of Raymond Roger Trencavel later that year a northern baron, Simon de Montfort, was declared Viscount. He took over the Trencavel lands as well as command of the invading army. The war dragged on for years with some extremely savage episodes in it. De Montfort was killed at the siege of Toulouse in 1218. The end came in 1244 with the fall of Montsegur Castle and the burning alive of the 144 Cathars captured there who refused to give up their faith.

Before entering the *Cité* by the *Porte Narbonaise*, it's worth taking a ride either in the small tourist train or in a *caleche*, a horse-drawn carriage, along the *lices* to see just how extensive the walls are. Later you can walk along part of the ramparts. Once you have passed over the drawbridge and through the barbican, head up the lane to the

Count's castle, a perfect example of medieval military architecture. There are guided tours usually on the hour or you can explore it on your own. The castle is open from 09.30-18.30 April – September, and 09.30-17.00 the rest of the year.

A short walk down Rue Saint Louis is the Basilica of St Nazaire, begun in 1096 in Romanesque style by the Trencavals and completed in Gothic style two hundred years later by the King of France. It has two singularly beautiful rose windows from the 13th and 14th centuries in the north and south transepts. There is more 13th century stained glass in two of the chapels. The organ which dates from 1522 is the finest in the south of France and free recitals are given at 17.00 every Sunday from mid June to mid September. Not far from the cathedral is the *Porte d'Aude* – see bottom left on the previous page. It is certainly worth walking through and going a short way down the hill to appreciate what a marvellous defence it was.

When you are ready to eat, the *Place Marcou* is ringed by brasseries and restaurants with many more in the streets nearby. You can spend an enjoyable half hour simply browsing menus and comparing prices which

are always displayed outside the restaurant. Inevitably the quality is variable, so check to see if there are any recommendations listed such as Routard or Michelin.

Afterwards, there are several shops worth a look inside, selling lace and tapestry work, linen goods, wooden toys, locally made sweets, regional delicacies, and the wares of potters and wood turners and metalworkers. There is a book shop with a good selection in English about the *Cité* and about the Cathars, but many of the shops are simply outlets for picture postcards and souvenirs,

soft drinks and ices.

There are a few small museums mostly about different aspects of life in the Middle Ages. Children will enjoy the *Musée de la Chevalerie* with all its weapons and the *Musée Mémoires du Moyen Age* about life here particularly at the time of the siege in 1240 when supporters of the Trencavels tried to recapture the *Cité*. The *Musée de l'Ecole* at 3 *rue de Plo* about school life in the late 19th and early 20th century can be of interest for young and old alike (see page 23).

Despite the crowds of tourists in summer, the *Cité* is a wonderful place to visit. Reckon on spending half a day or longer in it. Arrive early morning and you will avoid the crowds. It is just about accessible for wheel-chairs but difficult especially at the Narbonne Gate.

One minor negative comment: the public toilets are not always clean and they often lack paper. The toilets in a café or restaurant are likely to be better.

Find out more about the *Cité* at www.carcassonne-tourisme.com and at www.carcassonne.culture.fr

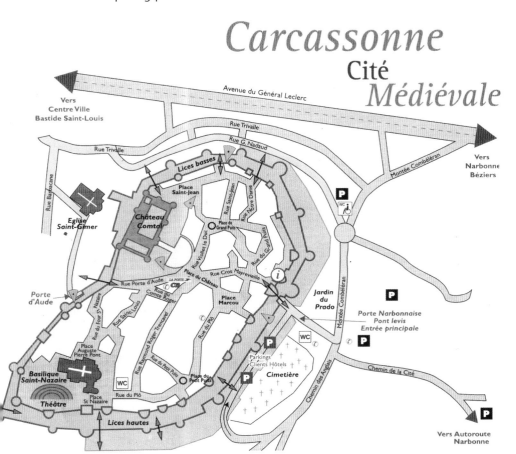

Carcassonne Cité Médiévale

Carcassonne – *La Bastide* the lower city

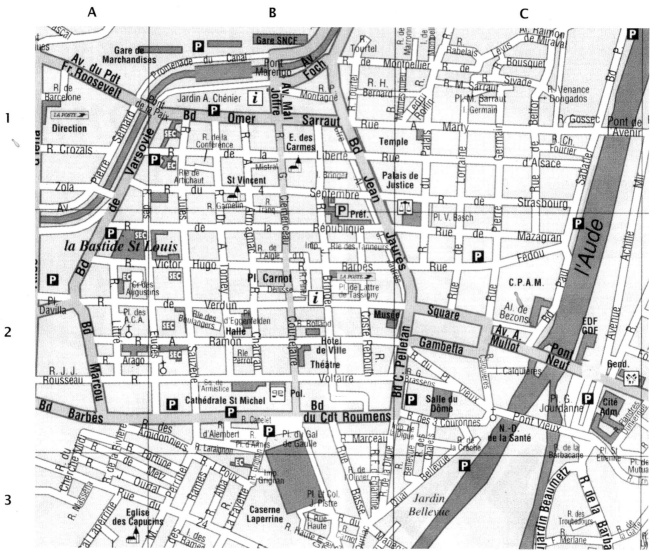

The shuttle bus (*navette*) will take you from the Narbonne Gate down to the lower city stopping outside the railway station which is by the *Canal du Midi* and the André Chénier Gardens – see the above **Town Map B1**. If you prefer to walk, exit by the Aude Gate and go down the hill over the 14th century *Pont Vieux* heading for the walls of the *Bastide* St Louis, the city built on the orders of King Louis in 1247 after he had annexed the region. If you are driving, follow the signs for *centre ville*. There are underground car parks at Square Gambetta, by the André Cheniér Gardens and under *Place du General de Gaulle*. There is plenty of parking along *Boulevard Barbès* which is free during the lunch hours of 12 - 14.00.

The heart of the *bastide* which is built to a draught board layout is the *Place Carnot* - **Town Map B2**. Its centrepiece is a large, baroque fountain depicting Neptune built by an Italian sculptor in the 18th century. The base of the fountain as well as the pavements around the square are laid with the distinctive red marble from Caunes Minervois. A market is held in the square on Tuesdays, Thursdays and Saturdays in the morning. It is especially good on Saturdays – stalls piled high with fresh, local, seasonal produce: peaches, melons, asparagus, olives, nuts, all kinds of vegetables, flowers, home-made bread, honey, cheeses, and much else. Nearby is *les Halles*, the indoor market for fresh fish and meat, and now also home to a sculpture exhibition.

There are 8 café-bars and brasseries around the square, and their tables and sunshades cover the square in summer. In the surrounding streets you will find a number of small restaurants where you can enjoy a three course set lunch for 12-18 euros; try the *Au bon Pasteur* on *Rue Armagnac* or *L'Endroit* on *rue de l'Aigle d'Or*. If you don't want a full meal there are *patisseries* selling mouth watering pastries and cakes, and take-away pizza places and pancake shops where you can also buy soft drinks.

There is a good range of shops including some elegant clothes boutiques and a very fine, old-style grocer *La Ferme* at 55 *rue de Verdun* which is one of the main shopping streets. Another is the pedestrianised *rue Georges Clemenceau* which runs from the square up to the station, and the *rue Barbès*. If you need to read your e-mails, there is an internet café *Alerte Rouge* at 73 *rue de Verdun* and another at 32 *rue de la Re-publique, Call World*, which also has network and educational games for children aged over 12.

Outside estate agents, of which there are many, you can pick up free copies of their monthly magazines listing properties for sale, tempting visitors to move down here. Though be warned, the days of buying an old property in need of restoration at a bargain price are almost gone. You might, however, be lucky!

A short walk away from *Place Carnot* is the Cathedral of St Michel – **Map B2**. Built as a parish church in the 13th and 14th centuries, it became the cathedral of the diocese in 1803. Following a fire in 1849 it was renovated by Viollet le Duc, the man responsible for the restoration of the *Cité*. St Vincent's Church on the *rue Armagnac* dating from 1242 is a fine example of Gothic architecture and has the second widest nave in France. An informative leaflet about all 7 of the town's ancient churches is available called 'Discovering the religious heritage of Carcassonne'.

There are some fine 18th century private mansions (called 'hôtels' in French but they are not hotels!); the Museum of Fine Arts is housed in one of them, the Presidial, at 1 *rue de Verdun*. Its permanent collection is mostly of 18th and 19th century French, Dutch and Italian artists and it has a whole room of paintings done by the Carcassonne artist Jacques Gamelin (1738-1803). It also hosts excellent, temporary exhibitions and is occasionally the

venue for concerts especially by local musicians. Entry to the museum is free – open 10.00 -17.00 every day during the summer. There is also a score of galleries and other places hosting photo and art exhibitions.

The town's oldest mansion is the *Maison du Senéchal* at 70 *rue Aimé Ramond*, the former residence of the King's ruling representative which

dates from the 13th century.

During the summer there are free guided tours of the Lower City starting from the tourist office which is at 28 *rue de Verdun*. Audio guides (3€) are available for hire there all year. The city's main tourist website provides a monthly list of every kind of entertainment and activity, including sport. The *Bastide* festival in July presents around 70 free shows and concerts, often held in the André Cheniér Gardens which is where a market of local crafts and regional foods is held on Sunday mornings from mid July to mid September. You can get further details from the main tourist office. For the more sporty, there is a water jousting tournament in late September and full and half marathons in October.

A lovely way to spend a lazy after-noon digesting lunch is to take the short boat trip along the *Canal du Midi* from the harbour by the André Cheniér Gardens. These canal boat trips run from May to November.

If you are feeling more energetic, you can hire a bike nearby (8 euros for half a day) at ESPACE 11, 3 *route Minervois* and cycle along the old, tree-shaded towpath which runs alongside the canal. Buy a baguette and some cheese and wine and enjoy a picnic in the sunshine by one of the locks, watching the cruisers entering and leaving them. Bliss!

See www.carcassonne.org

Castles: 'The Sons of Carcassonne'

The Pope launched a crusade in 1209 against the Cathars or *Bon Hommes* living in this region. They were regarded as heretics and a danger to the Catholic Church. Following the capture by the Crusaders of Béziers, Bram, Carcassonne, Lastours, Minerve, and other places harbouring Cathars and the execution of prisoners holding that faith, the survivors found refuge in a number of mountain top castles of which the most famous is Montsegur. The last to hold out was Quéribus which was handed over to the King of France's seneschal in 1255. Five of these castles were known as the 'Sons of Carcassonne': Puilaurens, Termes, Aguilar, Peyrepertuse and Quéribus, all of them situated to the south of Carcassonne and originally meant to protect the borders of the kingdom of Aragon.

They are often incorrectly called 'Cathar Castles'. They were in fact simply castles belonging to local nobles who allowed Cathars to find sanctuary in them. Two in the 'must be seen' category are Quéribus and Peyrepertuse. Fortunately both are

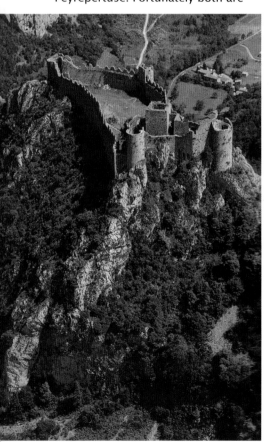

situated within sight of each other in the Corbières hills. There is an entrance fee at most of the castles – usually about €5 for adults and €2 for children.

Puilaurens Centre page map C4, pictured bottom left, stands guardian at a height of 690 metres over the pass that leads towards the upper valley of the Aude. It is a steep climb up a forest track from the car park above the village of Lapradelle-Puilaurens but there are substantial remains to see once you get there, including a keep and some fine crenallated walls. There are magnificent views from the battlements. It is well worth a visit. A few of the surviving Cathar *parfaits* found refuge here in 1245 after the fall of Montsegur.

Aguilar Map E3 is situated on a small hill near Vingrau with fine views over the *garrigue*. It was originally a Catalan stronghold. It consists of an older, inner pentagonal keep around which octagonal walls were built about the end of the 13th century long after the Crusade against the Cathars.

Termes Map D3
Little remains of this castle whose lord, Raymond de Termes, was a supporter of the Cathars and gave them sanctuary. It was besieged by the northern army in 1210 and the garrison was killed when they tried to flee.

Quéribus Map D4 pictured top right, has a spectacular location, balanced on a pinnacle of rock and standing above a sheer cliff. No wonder it was never captured! There are breath-taking views from its roof across to the Pyrenees in the south, away to the coast in the east, and inland over vineyards and villages to Peyrepertuse in the distance on its high, rocky perch. The castle is a 20 minutes walk from the car park and then a steep climb up to the outer walls. Among its several attractions is a fine vaulted Gothic keep. Audio guide tapes are available for hire. Find out more about special events there in the summer at www.queribus.fr

Peyrepertuse Map D3 pictured below is perched on a long narrow mountain ridge 800 metres up and with drops of hundreds of metres on three sides. It makes a most dramatic skyline. On very windy days or during an electrical storm, standing on its walls is no place to be! 300 metres long by 50 wide, it is the largest of all these mountain top

sanctuaries; spacious enough to have room for a small village at the lower level plus a chapel built in 1115. Many of those who survived Trencavel's unsuccessful attempt to recapture Carcassonne in 1240 sought refuge here but failed to hold the castle, surrendering after a two month siege by King Louis'seneschal. The upper part of the castle is an additional fortification built after it became French. Be warned – it is a steep climb from the car park to the castle. You can get a particularly fine view of the castle and the limestone cliff on which it stands from the village of Cucugnan.

A four day medieval festival is held here in early August at which the Knights of Peyrepertuse *Les Frères d'Armes* take part in jousting. In the spring and summer there are also displays of falconry. Find out more at www.chateau-peyrepertuse.com

At Montfernier Belvédère near **Lastours Map C1** there is a look out point which gives a panoramic view across to the four castles, pictured above right, before you descend to the village in the valley of the river Orbiel and then start the steep climb up to them. A *son et lumière* production is staged in July and August which can be watched from an enclosed area with seats at Belvédère. The remains of the medieval village which was probably deserted about 1240 have been excavated and the finds are now on display in an archaeological exhibition *Lastours, 4000 ans d'histoire*. There is also a gastro-nomic restaurant there called *Le Puits du Trésors*.

There are also the remains of castles at **Saissac Map B1** and **Arques Map C3** where Cathars found refuge during the Crusade. And at **Villerouge Terménès Map D3** pictured below, where Guilhem Bélibaste, the last Cathar *parfait* to be burned at the stake died in 1321. The castle belonged at that time to the Archbishop of Narbonne though the only time he ever visited it was to witness Bélibaste's execution. There is a permanent audiovisual exhibition in this castle about Catharism and the power of the Catholic Church in the 14th century. It has an added attraction in the form of *La Rôtisserie Médiévale* where you can eat medieval style.

At **Puivert Map B3** there is a 14th century castle with a keep 35 metres high and a main courtyard. See www.chateau-de-puivert.com

The Aude Tourist Board has a good, free 16 page publication called 'Catharism' which gives a brief account of each castle. All of them are well worth visiting. See www.tourisme. corbieres-minervois.com

Montsegur Map A3 across the border in the *département* of Arièges is more famous because of the Cathars 'last stand' there with its savage outcome in 1244 but the ruins which postdate the crusade are not, in my judgement, as exciting and evocative as some of those situated in the Corbières hills which are pictured on the previous page. See www.aude-tourisme.com

Medieval Abbeys and Churches

Religion affected every aspect of life in the Middle Ages and the Roman Catholic Church had a monopoly in Western Europe. A chapel or church was to be found in almost every village in this region. The monastic orders were major landowners and the remains of their abbeys can still be seen. Some of them stand as silent witnesses to a bygone age but others are still in use as parish churches. Here is a selection of the best but you will find that many a village has a medieval church not listed here which is worth seeing.

Several of the major churches have stone carving done by a brilliant 12th century itinerant craftsman whose work is to be seen as far afield as northern Spain and Tuscany in Italy. Sadly his name is not known. He is referred to now as the Master of Cabestany, the name of a small village near Perpignan, in whose church a magnificent timpanum carved by him was discovered in 1930 which provoked international interest in his work. So far 120 sculptures by him have been identified. Examples of his work are to be found at Lagrasse, St Hilaire, St Papoul and Rieux Minervois.

Lagrasse Map D2 is listed among *Les Plus Beaux Villages de France* and deservedly so for its setting, its picturesque, narrow medieval streets and market place, a hump-backed bridge over the River Orbieu dating from the 12th century and its Abbey,

pictured below, which was founded as a Benedictine community in 799, and dedicated to St Mary.
See www.lagrasse.com

Caunes-Minervois Map D1 is famous for its marble quarries and for its 8th century abbey church, pictured right, dedicated to Saints Peter & Paul. It has a fine crypt open to the public, a 12th century sculpted Norman doorway, cloisters, conventual buildings and a three-storey bell tower. It has a well stocked reception and sales room, and has several small exhibitions of art, marble artefacts, prehistoric pottery found locally and pieces of carved stonework including a sarcophagus from the 12th century. It hosts a series of classical concerts on Friday evenings during the summer. It serves now as the town's parish church whose clergy are Benedictine monks.

Saint Papoul Map B1 is named after the 4th century evangelist to this area. This imposing, fortified Benedictine abbey was founded in the 8th century. The church dates from the 12th century and the cloisters were rebuilt in the 14th. It is rich in stone carvings done by the Master of Cabestany and there is an exhibition of the sculptor's work in the refectory, showing plaster casts and photographs of his work done elsewhere. The reception area houses a nice selection of cards and books.

Rieux-Minervois Map D1 The village's parish church which dates from the 12th century is architecturally unique in France being seven-sided. Its ambulatory has 14 capitals with some exceptional stone carvings such as the one of the Assumption of the Blessed Virgin Mary pictured below. There is also a striking, multi-coloured represent-ation of Christ being laid in the tomb. It is attributed to the Burgundy School dating from the 15th century.

Saint Hilaire Map C2 is another Benedictine fortified abbey founded in the 8th century. The present church was begun in Romanesque style at the end of the 12th century and has a 13th century Gothic nave with the reliquary of the martyr St. Sernin, the first Bishop of Toulouse, carved in the form of a sarcophagus from a single block of Pyrenean white marble by the Master of Cabestany. It is a masterpiece! The superb Gothic cloisters, pictured below, have 54 arches dating from the 14th century. The Chapter House has very fine groin vaulting painted at the beginning of the 16th century and restored in 1860. St Hilaire ceased being a monastic community in 1748 and 10 years later the bishop designated the abbey church as the parish church. As well as being the burial place of the Counts of Carcassonne, St Hilaire is also the birthplace of the oldest sparkling wine in the world. Blanquette de Limoux was invented by the monks at the abbey in 1531.

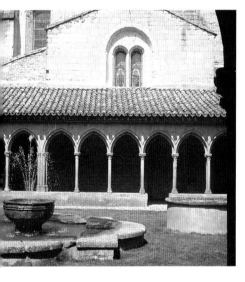

The abbey at **Fontfroide Map E2**, pictured top right, was founded as a Benedictine community in 1093. Following a visit by St Bernard to the Languedoc in 1145, it became affiliated to the Cistercians and soon became one of that order's greatest abbeys in Europe. One of its former monks was Pierre de Legate, whose murder in 1208 provoked the Pope into calling for a crusade against the Cathars. The abbey was a bastion of Catholic orthodoxy in the long-running conflict with Catharism. After the French Revolution the monastic buildings were confiscated and sold to various landowners but all were preserved. In 1908 Gustave and Madeleine Fayet bought the site in an auction sale and began the work of

renovation which is still being done by their descendants today.

Since 1909 it has hosted many painters and musicians and is still a centre for classical music. It has extensive rose gardens with 3,000 rose trees. It also boasts a fine restaurant and there is a picnic area. The abbey's own estate wine and other local produce along with many books about monasticism are on sale in the abbey shop. If you are feeling energetic after your visit, there is pleasant walking on the surrounding *massif de Fontfroide*. And some of the paths lead directly up the hillside above the abbey. Visitors can freely walk the land around the abbey but entrance to all the monastic buildings is only permitted as part of a guided tour which costs 9€ for adults and 2€ for children. The tour lasts about one and a half hours. The guides speak only French and they do give a long, detailed commentary.
See www.fontfroide.com

Villelongue Map B1 near St Papoul has a former Cistercian abbey dating from the 12th century with a cloister from the beginning of the 14th and it has some very pretty gardens. It is now privately owned and is gradually being restored but much remains to be done. Art exhibitions and concerts are held in the refectory and it hosts an annual gourd festival in September.

There is an 11th century abbey at **St Polycarpe Map C3** near St Hilaire, and at **Alet les Bains Map C3** there are extensive ruins of a former

cathedral with monastic buildings from the 12th-14th centuries.

You will find many more architecturally significant churches in the region such as the one at **St Martin des Puits Map D3** which has some well preserved 12th century frescoes and a pre-Norman chancel or the tiny 12th century chapel dedicated to St Sernin in the Montagne Noire pictured below – **Map C1**. The RC Diocese of Carcassonne and Narbonne has published an excellent illustrated guide to seven Church Trails taking in the best of the medieval ecclesiastical architecture in Aude. The title of the guide is *Balades en Pays d'Aude Itineraires touristiques du patrimonie religieux audeois*.

The Canal du Midi

This is the second UNESCO World Heritage Site in the *département* of Aude. Built between 1666 and 1681 it links the Mediterranean Sea with the Atlantic Ocean. It was built originally to be a mercantile waterway taking the produce of the southern Languedoc region and imports from other Mediterranean lands to the Atlantic for export. It runs from the port of Sète to the city of Toulouse where it meets up with the River Garonne which flows westwards to Bordeaux and the Gironde Estuary. The Canal featured in the 2005 BBC series *French Odyssey* when the TV chef Rick Stein travelled its length sampling the local fare and creating some dishes of his own.

The man with the vision and determination to carry out this monumental task was a salt tax inspector in Béziers called Pierre-Paul Riquet. The idea of such a canal had been around since Roman times but the problems of creating a waterway through hilly terrain and without an adequate water supply in the dry season had prevented it being realised. Riquet believed he knew how to do it and he persuaded King Louis XIV to back it. His plan involved the creation of a large artificial lake, the St Ferriol Reservoir **Map B1**, in the Montagne Noire to provide a constant water supply for the highest reaches of the canal 50 miles away. The water from the mountains feeds the canal at Narouze where the watershed between the Atlantic and the Mediterranean lies. Here an obelisk in memory of Riquet was erected in 1825 by his family.

When royal, financial support ran out, he used his and his wife's personal fortunes to continue the work, beggaring himself in the process. It took a labour force of 12,000 men 15 years to complete the immense task. Riquet died, ill and exhausted, just months before it was finished.

It runs for 240 km (150 miles), has 64 locks, and 54 aquaducts, some to re-route rivers across it, the longest of which is the 190 metre

long Aquaduct de l'Orb. One of Riquet's most impressive engineering feats (remember this man was a tax collector by profession, not a civil engineer) is the Malpas Tunnel. Instead of skirting round the Ensérune Hill, he chose to tunnel 173 metres through it. It was an amazing feat for the time. The canal served successfully as a mercantile route for more than 200 years but eventually with the coming of the railway it ceased to be used for transporting goods.

One of the bargemen's overnight stops was at Le Somail which is still used for this purpose by holiday-makers. The village even has a grocer's shop on a barge, pictured below, moored by the towpath. For bibliophiles it also has a *librairie ancienne*, an antiquarian bookshop, with 50,000 books in stock.

Initially the route of the canal by-passed Carcassonne to the north but this was rectified at the end of the 18th century. By then the canal had already become a route to be followed for pleasure too, and this

is what it is now. Hundreds of large and small houseboats and cabin cruisers ply its waters giving pleasure to tens of thousands of tourists every summer. The towpaths for the barges' horses have now become the preserve of early morning joggers, and walkers and cyclists. If you would like to cycle the length of the canal, an English couple based at Paraza **Map E2** near Argens-Minervois provide a service for such cyclists.
See www.mellowvelos.com

The canal provides a slow, relaxing way of exploring the region, and not least of sampling wines from the scores of vineyards that are passed en route. The speed limit on the canal is just 5mph. There is no requirement for a sailing licence on the canal, but before taking control of a hire boat, you will be shown how to manoeuvre it and how to work the locks if there is no lock keeper. There are plenty of places to tie up for the night, such as here in Carcassonne, pictured on the right, and the bigger places offer a variety of facilities for boats. In September there are boat tournaments on the canal at Carcassonne. One of the busiest spots on the canal is the port in Castelnaudary. The *bassin* there is very broad which makes turning boats round easy.

Boats can be hired for just a day or longer at a number of centres along the canal, including Homps **Map D1**, Le Somail **Map E1/2**, Trèbes **Map C2**, Carcassonne **Map C2** and Castelnaudary **Map B1**. Or you can take a *promenade en bâteau* for a couple of hours from either Homps or Carcassonne; a running commentary is given by a guide in French, English and Spanish about the history of the canal and its fauna and flora, and as you pass through locks you see at first-hand how they are operated.

To give an idea of prices – a two hour cruise from Homps along the route illustrated costs 10€ for an adult and 5.50€ for children aged between 3 and 13. Alternatively you could hire a cruiser for 12 people for 200€ for a full day.

You can also hire electrically powered boats by the hour or half day at La Redorte **Map D2** and at Port de Bram **Map B2** See www.castelnautique.com

The *Aire de Port Lauragais* **Map A1**, a motorway rest area, on the A61 between Toulouse and Carcassonne is on the same site as a marina on the canal close to the watershed at Narouze. It has a cultural centre dedicated to Riquet which has an informative exhibition about the canal.

A newly opened attraction is the *Musée et Jardins du Canal du Midi* in the original home of Pierre-Paul Riquet close to the *Bassin de St Ferréol* **Map B1** in the Montagne Noire. The museum is set in a park laid out in the 19th century. It is a beautiful forested area with some lovely walks.

One of the Aude Tourist Board's brochures is about *tourisme fluvial*, more particularly the *Canal du Midi et de la Robine*. It lists all the places where you can hire boats and cycles, as well all the short boat trips along sections of the canal. See www.vnf.fr and www.audetourisme.com Another very informative website is www.midicanal.fr

Plan de Situation

Wine Trails

The whole *département* of Aude is covered in vineyards. Despite the big drop in consumption of wine by the French (and a consequent drop in the number of road fatalities thanks also to a policy of stricter controls on drink-driving), winemaking remains the major industry in the region with several hundred vineyards producing eight *appellations controlées*. The Languedoc was once known for the vast quantities of cheap, low quality wine it produced. It is still the largest producer in France but the quality over the past decade and more has risen significantly and the best of its wines now compare favourably with the best from other regions and remain cheaper. The *AOC* (*l'appellation d'origine controlée*) quality wines are: **Cabardès, Corbières, Fitou, Limoux, Malepère, Minervois** and **Muscat de RIvesaltes. La Clape**, the peninsula near Narbonne and the neighbouring area of **Quatourze** are now marketed as **Coteaux Languedoc**. In addition, winegrowers in the area close to the city of Carcassonne produce very good *Vins de Pays*. You will also find *Vins de Pays de l'Aude* and *Vins de Pays d'Oc*.

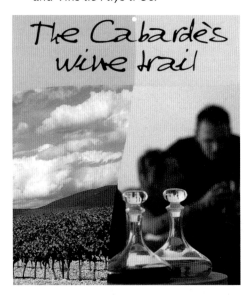

Wines vary considerably depending on a whole range of factors of which climate (sunshine, wind, and humidity) is an important one – **Cabardès**, for example, has two vintages: Atlantic (using Merlot and Cabernet grapes) and Mediterranean (using Syrah and Grenache grapes). This is true also of the **Malepère** wines. The soil's mineral content is another major determining factor as well as the age of the vines, the mix of grapes and the individual skills of the winemakers. This all makes for some interesting, even exciting wine tasting. You can, of course, simply browse the wine shelves in a hypermarket and pick a selection at random to try and find the ones you might enjoy and want to take a supply home with you. Much more enjoyable, however, is to tour part of the region and stop at a number of vineyards, meet with those who make the wine, taste a tiny glass or two and buy a couple of bottles at each place when you find ones you particularly like. The important words to look out for as you drive along are: *Cave* or *Caveau*, *Degustation* and *Vente* meaning wine cellar, wine tasting and wine for sale.

You might also like to visit one of the bigger specialist retailers or the showplace for a particular *AOC*, such as the one for **Minervois** wines at Le Chai-Port Minervois at Homps **Map D1**, pictured below, where you can get advice on over a hundred wines of the Minervois region. Every Tuesday and Thursday from 16.00 to 19.00 during the summer there are lectures at the Chai given by local winemakers who share their knowledge and enthusiasm with visitors. They hold a *Foire aux Rosés* during the second week of June and this is just one of several wine promotions at the Chai.

The local weekly paper *Le Semaine du Minervois* publishes a free wine guide to Minervois wines called *Quelle Vins acheter/ Which Wines to buy?* It is quite informative about such things as what varieties of grapes are used and what combinations are permitted in an *AOC* wine but its usefulness is limited as it covers only 16 of the wine villages and only a few of the vineyards in each of those villages. One immediate lesson to be learnt from it, however, is that you need to do a lot of tasting to appreciate the full range and diversity of wines within a single *appellation*. What an enjoyable prospect!

Detailed Wine Trail brochures for the various *AOCs* are readily available in the tourist offices. They can help you decide which route you would like to follow and which vineyards you would like to visit.

The **Minervois** region extends from the Montagne Noire in the north to the *Canal du Midi* in the south and the *Cité* in the west and is about 5,500 hectares in size. It is a real mosaic of landscapes with eight distinct sectors identified where a wide variety of grapes are grown. The village of La Lavinière **Map D1** has its own *appellation communale* **Minervois La Lavinière (AOC Village)** as does the village of St Jean-de-Minervois **Map E1** just over the departmental border which produces a wonderful sweet dessert wine: **Le Muscat de St-Jean-de-Minervois (Vin Doux Naturel).**

Corbières There are currently more than a hundred winegrowers in this region which covers an area of over 6,500 hectares stretching from Carcassonne across the Corbières hills to the south. An informative *Carte-guide à la découverte des Corbières* which lists sights to see and where you can eat or stay in the area is available from tourist offices. There is also a local high-quality *AOC* called **Corbières-Boutenac**. Find out more at www.aoc-corbieres.com

This region is best known for its full-bodied reds to savour with meat dishes. One place to taste some of them is at Terra Vinea on a hill overlooking Portel-des-Corbières **Map E3**. The local tourist office rightly describes it as 'one of the most curious attractions' in the area. In a disused gypsum mine 80 metres underground about 1,500 barrels of local wine are maturing, produced by three co-operatives operating under the name of *Caves Rocbère*. There are guided tours (in French) followed

by wine tasting. Also in the mine is an exhibition of tools used in wine making, a cooper's workshop and a mock Roman villa! See www.terra-vinea.com

The **Fitou** vineyards which produce intense, fragrant red wines stretch from the steep hillsides of the southern Corbières to the coast where the village of Fitou lies **Map E3**. The village has its annual wine festival at the end of July. The nine villages of the *appellation* also produce an excellent *AOC* sweet wine called **Muscat de Rivesaltes**. See www.cru-fitou.com and www.vinsdoux-aude.com

Limoux Map C2 was famous for its sparkling white wines long before Champagne and it still provides a very acceptable and much cheaper alternative to it. Benedictine monks at the Abbey of St Hilaire produced the world's first *brut* in 1531, *Blanquette de Limoux* – a blend primarily of Mauzac, with some Chenin and Chardonnay, aged for at least 8 months after a complex production process. *Crémant de Limoux* is a variation of the same with more Chenin and Chardonnay. *Blanquette Mèthode Ancestrale* is a low alcohol (7%) variation using 100% Mauzac grapes. The *Sieur d'Arques* winery in Limoux which produces six million bottles of sparkling wine a year offers a short teaching session on wine tasting. A major annual event is the wine auction *Toques et Cloches* in Limoux at the beginning of April which attracts over a thousand buyers in the wine and restaurant trade. Each year the auction funds structural repairs to one of the local parish churches. Find out more at www.limoux-aoc.com

If you would like to have a couple of hours tutoring in wine tasting by an English Master of Wine, Matthew Stubbs offers this at the impressive Domaine Gayda **Map B2** at Brugairolles near Limoux. He also shows how the wines of this region in France can challenge the best of the rest. His tutored tasting costs 30 euros per person. See his wine school website: www.vinecole.com

Some *vignerons* provide *chambres d'hôtes*, B + B, or even better the option of Dinner, B + B. One of the best meals I have ever had in

France was at *Les Fontanelles* near Puichéric where our host provided either a wine from his own vineyard or from a neighbour's for each of the five delicious courses his wife had prepared that evening for guests staying at their very comfortable *chambres d'hôtes*. In the course of the meal we were given a running commentary on the distinctive qualities of each wine and we learnt something about the whole process of wine-making. It was a memorable experience.

Check with the tourist office in Carcassonne if there are to be any *balades vigneronnes* whilst you are down there. This is a programme of visits to particular vineyards in the area where you will be taken on a two hour guided walk of the land followed by wine tasting and a meal. Advance booking is essential.

If you are here in the autumn you might be able to attend one of the village wine festivals. The **AOC Minervois La Lavinière**, for example, has its on a Saturday near the end of October. A typical day's programme would start with a wine tasting at 10.30, followed at 12 by a buffet lunch with wines of the *appellation*. At 15.00 there would be a guided walk led by winemakers of the village and in the evening there would be music and dancing. A bonus is that artists exhibit their work at some of the vineyards.

A lovely souvenir you can take home with you along with your bottles of wine is the free 40 page booklet published by the Aude Tourist Board called 'Vines, Wines and Winemakers'. It is not on display in the tourist offices so you will have to ask for a copy.

Recreational Areas & Outdoor Activities

If you are staying inland, you do not need to drive all the way to the coast to go swimming or wind-surfing. There are lakes with good recreational facilities much nearer. The closest is *Le Lac de la Cavayère* Map C2, pictured right, just 3 km from the *Cité*, known to some as Carcassonne Plage as it has sandy beaches. It is a beautifully landscaped reservoir created in 1988 following a fire in the area. There is a broad path around the lake's perimeter and the walk takes between one and two hours depending on your level of fitness. Along the way there are several small picnic areas with benches and tables in the shade of trees. Swimming is permitted but only in designated areas where there are lifeguards. You can hire pedaloes and canoes, play mini golf, or you can relax while the children enjoy themselves at the *02Aventure parcours acrobatique forestier*, a high level forestry acrobatic course which is open to the public from 13.00 to 20.30. In the morning it is reserved for groups of more than eight people who have booked in advance. Orienteering, mountain bike riding and horse riding are all allowed, and you can hire horses from the *Centre équestre*.

It is easy to find the lake – take the D6113 out of Carcassonne heading in the direction of Narbonne and before Trèbes turn right on to the road signposted to the lake.

Bus number 1 also goes there from Carcassonne.

Lapradelle Map C1 in the Montagne Noire provides similar facilities for walking and swimming and picnics, pictured top right next page. It has extensive parking close to the lake, toilets and a small café. Also in the Montagne Noire is the *Bassin de St Ferriol*, the main feed reservoir for the *Canal du Midi*. It is a beautiful spot with plenty of water activities: wind surfing, canoeing, sailing and pedaloes and the village has a number of cafés and restaurants. You can also go pony trekking through the forests of the Montagne Noire; contact *Domaine de l'Albejot* for information on 04 68 24 44 03.

Lake Jouarre Map D1 lies between Homps and Olonzac and is one of the biggest expanses of inland water. A holiday village has been developed nearby. Swimming is permitted and lifeguards are on duty in the summer. There is a sailing school, and dinghies can be hired. The path alongside the *Canal du Midi* which runs close to

the lake is great for cycling. Bikes can be hired from Homps.

Heading south from Carcassonne in the direction of the Pyrenees offers other opportunities for outdoor activities. In Limoux you can join a canoeing expedition along the River Aude – see www.canoe limoux.com and further south at Quillan there is canyoning and whitewater rafting through the gorges on the River Aude. Contact *Centre International de Séjour La Forge* at Laforge@wanadoo.fr for more information. This is a residential centre which provides all the equipment necessary for the various outdoor activities. The one condition required of participants is that they can swim 250 metres. *Sud Rafting* based at Point d'Aliès Axat is another water activity centre with a lot on offer. You can contact them at sudrafting@ liberty-surf.fr Another centre with qualified leaders is *Audescapades* at Villasavary – for details, see www.audescapades.com. And one more, based at Puichéric, is L'eaurizon –see www.eau-rizon.org.

Le Lac Montbel Map B3, pictured above, in the Haute Vallée d'Aude offers wonderful walking, swimming and sailing. There is also a passenger boat that provides tours during the summer around the key access points and wildlife sites.

Horse and pony riding can be done at *Domaine de Pommayrac* (tel 04 68 69 49 60) in the village of Verzeille between Carcassonne and Limoux. All levels are catered for – beginners are taught by a qualified instructor and those at intermediate or advanced level are also supervised. There is pony riding for children aged 3 to 12. *La Gontarende* at Cuxac-Cabardès **Map C1** also offers pony trekking as well as tuition in horse riding. Open from 09.00 – 19.00. And you will find a Mini-Ranch on the outskirts of the village Villeneuve-Minervois **Map C1**. See www.centre-equestre-de-la-clamoux.com

Between Limoux and Quillan there is *ACCRO'Parc* at Alet-les-Bains **Map C3**. This is a forest trail high up in the trees, pictured below, – *Parcours Acrobatique Forestier.* Everyone has to do the beginners green trail under the direction of instructors in order to learn how to proceed through the trees safely; you then progress to the yellow trail which has 12 different games at a maximum height of 7 metres and finally to the red trail with 10 games between 4 and 10 metres above the ground.

If walking is among your favourite forms of exercise you will be spoilt for choice. Many of the villages have produced attractive, free leaflets describing walks in their immediate vicinity. *Laure Minervois* **Map D1**,

for example, has a full colour leaflet in English with notes about the historical sites you will pass if you follow the various suggested trails. The villages around Capendu in the commune of *Piemont d'Alaric* **Map D2** to the east of Carcassonne have produced a folder with 10 leaflets outlining routes for walks or bike rides in their area. In the south of the *département*, *Quercorb* **Map B3** and *Chalabre* have a colourful leaflet showing 15 walks of varying lengths.

A new guide for walkers in the Upper valley of the Aude is

le Pays de la haute Vallée de l'Aude which suggests 29 routes over the whole region. Even if you cannot read the commentary in French, you can still benefit from the very detailed maps.

The European walking route **GR 36** which runs from Switzerland to Spain passes through Aude from the oak forests of the Montagne Noire in the north along part of the *Canal du Midi* and on through the Corbières to the south. The route passes the castles at Villerouge Termenès, Termes and Peyre-pertuse. The Aude Tourist Board has published a free 24 page booklet about walking in the region and giving details of the maps you will need. It is called *Le Sentier Cathare Promenades et Randonnées*.

At the southern end of the *département* in *Aude en Pyrenees* there are 190 km of walking trails and 870 km of marked trails for mountain bikers, the largest such area in the Pyrenees. For more about the physical recreational facilities in the area, see www.aude-en-pyrenees.fr and www.vtt-pyrenees.com

Martyn and Ann Pickering who are themselves keen cyclists and walkers run an excellent service for those wanting an active holiday in this area. They also offer B + B at their home *Au Petit Verger* in Puivert. Their website is at www.cycleaude.com

Theme Parks & Animal Farms

Carcassonne has two major attractions of this kind. The first is just a few hundred metres from the *Cité* on a hillside at *La Colline de Pech-Mary*. It is called **La Cité des Oiseaux** – the city of birds. Here you can watch a 45 minute show as some of the world's most colourful birds display their aerial skills: African Maribou storks, crowned cranes, toucans and parrots as well as many kinds of birds of prey, among them eagles, condors, and falcons. There are more than 200 birds on site. In 2005, the city of birds was extended to include a mini farm and an enclosed area for wolves. From a raised observation point you watch the wolves coming to be fed with raw meat. The park is open to visitors from the end of March to the beginning of November, usually just from 14.00 – 18.00 but in July and August opening hours are extended to 10.30 – 12, and 14.30 – 18.30. There is a small shop where you can buy souvenirs of your visit. Entrance fee: 9€ for adults and 5€ for children under 12. Find out more from www.citedesoiseaux.com

The other attraction which is just five minutes away from the *Cité* in the direction of Lake Cavayère is **Le Parc Australien** where you can get a taste of life in Australia with its display of wildlife from that continent. There are supervised activities for children such as panning for gold, learning to throw a boomerang or play a didgeridoo and much more. In the summer it is open from 14.00 Monday to Saturday and from

11.00 on Sundays and during school holidays. Entrance costs 8€ for adults and 6€ for children. Out of season the park is open just on Wednesdays, Saturdays and Sundays from 14.00. Find out more at http://leparcaustralien.free.fr

Drive north from Carcassonne towards the Montagne Noire and you have a number of choices. Near Saissac **Map B1** at *Picarel le Haut*, Catherine Sonef has been farming deer since 1986 and now has some 450 animals. Entry and parking is free at this working farm from 10.00 – 12, and 14.00 – 19.00. There are guided tours at 15.00 and 17.00 costing just 2€ for adults, children under 10 are free. Many of the animals are very tame and will let you stroke them if you approach them quietly. The farm has its own simple shop and an auberge where you can enjoy a meal of *civet de daguet*, the succulent meat of very young stags bred there, accompanied by fresh vegetables, fruit and cheeses from neighbouring farms. See www.picarel-cerf.com

Near Castans **Map D1** on the Route de Pradelles (D9) in a beautiful forested area you can visit **Les Lamas de la Montagne Noire**. These gentle animals from Chile are now being bred here and you can go on a short trek along one of the woodland paths with one of them. If you book in advance you can ask to have an English speaking guide. See www.lamabalade.free.fr

By far the largest nature reserve is **La Réserve Africaine de Sigean Map E2** about 15 km south of Narbonne off highway D6009. Expect to spend at least half a day at it. There are over 3,800 animals on site from the continent of Africa – everything you would expect to see: elephants, giraffes, leopards, lions, rhinos, springboks, zebras and much more.

The visit falls into two parts: a six km drive through what are designated as savannah and bush areas where you can expect to see big game – the biggest are a quartet

of white rhinos – and then a two to three hour stroll which will take you past an island for chimpanzees, a small lake with flocks of flamingos, ibis, pelicans and many more species, and along the African plain dotted with lots of other wildlife, including buffalo and elephants.

This game reserve claims to have more Tibetan bears than are left in Tibet! You can expect to get some good, close up photos of the wild life – ostriches and zebras roam across the roads. There is a strict instruction to keep the car windows closed and never to get out of the car. Resist the temptation to lower a window and take a picture when you are driving close to the pride of lions!

The park has kiosks and a restaurant, as well as indoor and outdoor areas for picnics.

This is the most expensive of the animal parks and farms in the area: 25€ for adults and 19€ for children but it makes a great day out. The park is open every day of the year from 9.00 to 18.30 in the

summer and to 18.00 in the winter. For more details see www.reserveafricainsigean.fr

The *Parc historique de loisirs en terre Cathare* is a very different kind of theme park located at the *Château de Chalabre* Map B3 between Mirepoix and Limoux. An Association known as *Les Chevaliers du Kercorb* has been renovating the castle and its adjoining park since 2002 and the knights now give children the chance to learn about and to experience a wide variety of activities associated with life in the middle ages, among them archery, heraldry, watching the knights in the jousting tournaments, taking part in dancing and games, as well as less vigorous activities such as calligraphy and iconography.

It is open during the French school holidays at Easter and on Ascension Day, and during July and August from 12.00 – 18.30. Find out more at www.chateau-chalabre.com

Whilst not a theme park as such, lovers of falconry can see some impressive displays at Peyrepertuse castle **Map D3** – during the spring and summer. Check their website for details of dates and times. It is an important element in the *Festival Médiéval* held there in early August. When it started in 2003 the festival attracted 3,000 visitors, by 2005 that had risen to 12,000 and numbers continue to increase year by year. See www.chateau-peyrepertuse.com for details.

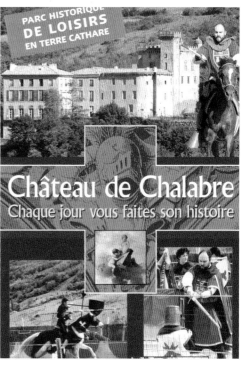

PARC HISTORIQUE
DE LOISIRS
EN TERRE CATHARE

Château de Chalabre
Chaque jour vous faites son histoire

Sun, Sea and Sand

This stretch of the Mediterranean coast gets over 300 days of sunshine a year and with an average of just 12 mm of rain in July and 30mm in August. So you are more or less guaranteed dry sunny weather. The truth, however, is that it can sometimes get too hot – temperatures of 35ºc/100ºf at midday are not unusual so it is advisable to stay out of the sun between 12 noon and 14.00 and to use high factor sun-screen when you are on the beach.

Most of the coastline is one long sandy beach or sandbar between the sea and inland lagoons, and the resort beaches have all won blue flag awards for their cleanliness. In the early 1960s the Government funded the construction of eight new holiday resorts along the Languedoc-Roussillon coast. The first task was to eradicate all the malarial mosquitoes which bred in the marshes and lagoons. At the same time care was taken to protect the natural environment and not destroy it by over development. Their initiative paid off as millions of French and foreign tourists now spend their summer vacations here but driving the A9 motorway at the start and end of the French national holidays in August can be hell. Be warned! Local papers publicise the days and times when the roads are likely to be most congested and suggest less trafficated routes.

The biggest resorts are just across the Aude borders, to the east at Cap d'Agde which boasts the largest naturist holiday village in Europe and to the west in Roussillon

at Canet Plage, St Cyprien and Argelès Plage which with its 60 campsites must be the biggest camping centre in Europe. But Aude too has its share of fine beaches and smaller resorts. Thousands of pine trees, tamarisk and laurels have been planted and much of the development is low-rise apartment blocks and holiday homes. Starting with Les Cabanes de Fleury on the edge of the La Clape massif, and running west in the direction of Spain, they are St Pierre-sur-Mer which merges into Narbonne Plage, Gruissan, Port-La-Nouvelle, La Franqui (the oldest seaside resort on the coast), Leucate Plage and Port Leucate. The last one together with its neighbour La Bacarès in Rousssillon have the largest yachting marinas on the Languedoc coast.

The best of these resorts is arguably **Leucate Plage Map F3**. The beach of fine sand runs for 8 km with the sea on one side and the lagoon, the *Etang de Leucate ou Salses*, on the other. Frequent winds make this long lagoon ideal for windsurfing and kite surfing. In fact the wind blows here on 300 days a year. What many might regard as an inconvenience, the local mayor back in 1996, Michel Py, decided to see as a blessing and since then they have been hosting the annual world championship in windsurfing. At the *Mondial du Vent* in April 2008 there were about 250 competitors and over 150,000 spectators – this year the dates are 11 – 19 April. See www.mondial-du-vent.com

The local council claims that *'les enfants sont rois'* and accordingly it arranges activities for children, many of them free. There are all the water sports and land based activities that you would expect to find, including a sailing school, boat trips, kite surfing, wind buggies for hire, and horse riding. You can take a two hour mini cruise in a 1930s schooner from Port Leucate. The resort also has four naturist colonies.

North of Leucate is **La Franqui**, a small family resort at the foot of some cliffs (a rare sight on this bit of the coast) which provides shelter from the *Tramontine* wind. Nearby is an immense, wild beach called Les Coussoules which is excellent for wind buggies. From the headland above La Franqui there are stunning views and this is a popular area for walking and mountain biking and even hang gliding. See www.leucate.net

If you need a break from the beach, the village of Fitou is close by where you can visit a lot of *caves* and sample their wines and it isn't far to the African Safari Park at Sigean or to the fortress, *Le Château de Salses*.

Port-La-Nouvelle Map F3 pictured above is very different. It was founded in 1820 as the commercial port for Narbonne to which it is linked by the *Canal de la Robine*. It is France's third largest port on the south coast and is the main one for handling fuel oil imports and distribution in the region. It also still has an active fishing fleet and fish market. Every morning from 9 you can buy freshly caught fish from the fishermen along the *Avenue de la Mer* (see below). You can watch freighters, tankers, and fishing boats as well as admiring the pleasure boats of the wealthy for it is a pleasure resort too. Quite a mix for one small town. There is a wide beach of fine white sand (cleaned every day) which slopes gently into the sea. The tourist office is conveniently located by a large car park at one end of the beach. In the height of the summer season canal boats run from Narbonne to Port la Nouvelle past the islands of Nadière and Sainte Lucie. The latter is now a 250 hectare heavily wooded nature reserve with a marked botanical trail. The town boasts an unusual attraction in the form of a whale's skeleton. The whale was washed up on the beach in1985 and a local wine maker with the help of family and friends towed it to his vineyard, *La Domaine de Jugnes*, on the outskirts of town where he cleaned and restored the 4 ton skeleton. It now serves as a free attraction tempting tourists to go and sample some of his wines. For more details see www.portlanouvelle.com

Gruissan Map F2 is different again. In the Middle Ages it served as one of Narbonne's ports. It is a picturesque, traditional village built in concentric circles round a hill topped by the *Tour de Barberousse*, the remains of a 13th century castle which was built for protection from Turkish pirates. Then there is the modern holiday resort with its beach apartment blocks, yachting marina and restaurants, and thirdly there is *La Plage des Pilotis* which was featured in the cult film *Betty Blue*. This is the site of a collection of 1300 wooden chalets built on piles to protect them from the sea which regularly covers the beach here. They were originally built as holiday homes at the end of the 19th century but were destroyed by the Germans in World War II. After the war exact replicas were built. An extra attraction this resort offers is deep sea fishing trips.

Nearby, salt extraction is done on a large scale on the Ile de St Martin – follow the signs for *Salin du Midi* from Gruissan old village. During the holiday season you can take a guided tour round the salt pans and buy some of this natural product. There is a small museum-cum-educational centre about 'farming' salt from Roman times.

The village also has an exhibition on bird migration and an observaion point in a protected area where you can watch the birds. Since 2004 the village has had a centre for training professionals in the wine industry and part of it is also open to the public. See www.ville-gruissan.com Wind surfing and kite surfing are popular pastimes here as elsewhere on the coast – see www.gruissan-windsurf.com

Narbonne Plage Map F2 is another modern, family resort with a vast, wide sandy beach and offering plenty of activities, including in the summer tuition in Salsa and Latin dancing on Tuesday evenings. The beach runs for five km along the coast to **St Pierre sur Mer**, once a small fishing harbour but also now a marina and a growing holiday resort. For information about kite- and windsurfing courses here see www.sudwindsports.com. The quieter end of this beautiful beach which shelves gently into the sea is just before the yachting marina on the edge of Narbonne Plage and St Pierre – see the picture below.

Nearby is the *Etang de Pissevaches* which is one of the *département's* finest ornithological sites where some 200 species of birds nest. Less peaceful and not far away is the water park Aquajet on the Route de Gruissan. See www.narbonne-plage.com

Museums with a Difference

Museums don't have to be boring! They can be fun and can certainly provide an entertaining and educational alternative when a break from the beach or the hills is needed. Here are a few suggestions which are worth a visit.

In the village of Villeneuve Minervois **Map C1**, ten miles north of Carcassonne the Bénazeth family restored a disused windmill dating from 1819 to full working order in 2002. It is the only functioning windmill in the *département* of Aude and during the 45 minute guided tour you can see it in action making flour. There is an exhibition about the mill's 19th century history and about the reconstruction work. The Bénazeth family are wine-makers and you can taste their products in the small shop at the reception centre. Their Plo de Roy vintage which is aged in oak barrels in the huge natural underground cavern, *le Gouffre de Cabrespine*, is particularly good. There is plenty of parking space by the mill and an attractive picnic area in what is a very pretty location. Open 10.00 – 18.30 in July and August and from 10.00 – 12.00 and 14.00 – 17.30 in May, June and September. Admission 5 € for adults, 3 € for children. See www.moulin-benazeth.fr

Le Musée de l'Ecole at 3 rue de Plô in the *Cité* will bring back memories to older visitors as it covers school life up to the middle of the 20th century, and French schools weren't that different to British ones before World War II. In addition to recreating school life a century ago

there is also a separate exhibition about France and her former colonies – some of which subsequently became British, notably Canada and India. Younger visitors will enjoy it too and may well appreciate their own very different school environment all the more when comparing it to how things were in their grandparents time. Open 10.00 – 18.00. This museum is accessible for visitors in wheelchairs.

Le Musée de la Chapellerie is at Le Somail **Map E2**, 7 miles to the north of Narbonne. If you love hats, this is the place to visit as it houses a vast collection of headwear from 84 countries. The oldest of the 6,500 exhibits dates back to 1850; the most recent additions are the headgear used by the army in the Gulf War. Details are given of their place of origin and usage: military, religious, ceremonial, etc. There are guided tours lasting an hour or you can choose to go at your own pace. Open 9.00 – 12.00 and 14.00 – 19.00 each day from June to September.

Le Musée Contemporain de la Chapellerie is another but quite different hat museum in the small town of Espéraza **Map C3** south of Limoux. A century ago it was the second largest manufacturer of hats in the world! Its 'golden age' was between the two World Wars when it had 14 factories employing over 4,000 people. Visitors are shown by means of video the whole process of hat making from the shearing of sheep right through to the finished and fashioned articles. And then they can inspect the many different machines which were once used in their manufacture. A range of hats are on sale. Open 10.00 – 12.00 and 14.00 – 18.00.

Right next door is *Dinosauria Le Musée des Dinosaures* and the entry charge covers both museums. In 2003 the remains of a hitherto unknown kind of dinosaur was

discovered in the neighbouring village of Campagne sur Aude and the museum shows an informative video about the excavation and subsequent reconstruction. There are a number of dinosaur remains on show as the region is rich in them. At Campagne **Map C3** there is a paleontological dig site with a fossil workshop for children. See www.dinosauria.org

Near Narbonne at 32 *quai de Lorraine* in the little wine village of Sallèles d'Aude **Map E2** beside the *Canal de Jonction* which links the *Canal du Midi* and the *Canal de la Robine* is the self-styled *Centre Européen du Patchwork*. It is housed in an old converted winery dating from the 19th century. There is a colourful and interesting permanent exhibition about the history, techniques and origins of patchwork, as well as temporary displays of the work of contemporary European artists – see below. If you would like to learn how to do patchwork, the Centre runs workshops and you can buy kits in the museum shop which also sells regional produce. It is open each day from 1st April to 1st November from 10.30 – 12.30 and 15.00 – 19.00. Open at weekends during the winter apart from January and February – see www.patchwork-cep.com

Also in the same village is **Amphoralis Musée des potiers gallo-romains**. This is an unusual museum in that it is built over a still unfinished archaeological dig. A clear explanatory leaflet in English plus photographs and models in the exhibition hall makes understanding the site straight forward. Archaeologists have uncovered pottery kilns and a settlement from Roman times. Over the past decade they have been reconstructing ovens for baking pottery modelled exactly on those unearthed. The work goes on and visitors can join in it on pre-published dates. Amphoras from here used in the export of wine from Narbonne have been found all over the Roman Empire – from Crete to northern Britain. The museum is open 1st July – 30th Sept 10.00 – 12.00 and 15.00 – 19.00. Opening hours are more restricted the rest of the year.

If you are planning to visit the attractive village of Montolieu

Map C1 which is France's equivalent to the original book town of Hay-on-Wye, there is a small museum about the world of writing. It is *le Musée du Livre Michel Braibant* which is dedicated to the art of writing and the printed word. Here you can learn all about the printing process, engraving, etching and binding. Open each day 10.00 – 12.00 and 14.00 – 18.00. And then there is *l'Atelier du Livre* where adults and children are invited to take part in workshops and learn how to produce their own books – everything from the paper to be used, typography, illustrations through to book binding – see www.atelierdulivre.net

Brousses **Map C1** where paper making was started in 1674 is a few miles to the north of Montolieu. *Le Moulin à papier de Brousses* is now in its 4th century of production and is a living, working museum where ancient techniques are still valued. The mill is in a lovely, wooded location but is not really accessible for those with limited mobility. Open all year. During July and August there are eight guided tours in French each day on the hour from 11.00 to 18.00, and five a day during September. For more information, see its website www.moulinapapier.com

Across the road from the railway station in Lezignan Corbieres **Map E2** is *le Musée de la vigne et du vin* which opened in 1973. It boasts a very large collection of tools and machinery from the past two centuries. The typical setting of a Languedocien wine maker in the 19th century has been recreated on a grand scale – it covers 1,400 sq metres and includes the courtyard, coopery, vinification cellar, barn, stables and tack room. You can, of course, do some wine tasting and buy other regional products. Open every day from 9.00 – 19.00.

Near the seaside village of Gruissan **Map F2** just off the D332 is *La Cité de la vigne et du vin* which was opened in 2004. The Centre houses a 500 sq metre exhibition (including an entertaining test of your sense of smell), a 5,000 sq metre grape variety garden and a greenhouse presenting the different stages in the development of the vine through the four seasons of the year. There is a lot to be learnt here about the history of wine making and

about the techniques used in its production, especially if you take part in a guided tour led by a professional oenologist. Open 10.00 – 20.00. See www.ville-gruissan.fr

Another specialist museum for those interested in history and music is *le Musée du Quercorb* at Puivert **Map B3** to the south of Limoux. In addition to the several rooms illustrating daily life in Quercorb in bygone times there is an Instrumentarium where you can see reconstructions of 8 musical instruments from the 14th century the details of which have been taken from stone carvings in the Castle's keep at Puivert! A video presentation tells how this was done and you can hear them being played. The museum is air conditioned and there is an attractive picnic area. Open from mid July to 31st August 10.00 –19.00, and from April to September 10.00 – 12.30 and 14.00 – 18.00. See www.quercorb. com/mus

If you are touring in the Montagne Noire and have children with you it is worth driving down on the northern side to the hamlet of Hautpoul near Mazamet just over the Aude border where you will find *le Maison du Bois et du Jouet*. They will love it. In addition to a fine museum about the forest and a collection of over 1,500 toys from all over the world, there are a number of wooden indoor games they can play. Outside there is a 'fairy tale trail' in the woods *Bois des Contes* where a series of small chalets have life size carved figures of the characters in the story depicted in that chalet. The setting at the foot of a cliff with a medieval village and castle on top is very impressive. And there is plenty of space for children to burn off surplus energy. Open 14.00 – 19.00. See www.hautpoul.org

Enjoying Nature

In order to enjoy the sight, scents and sounds of nature you don't need to be a well read amateur botanist or a keen ornithologist but it will certainly add greatly to your enjoyment if you gain some knowledge as you explore and discover just how bountiful nature is in this part of the Languedoc. A good French handbook is *La Nature Méditerrenéenne en France* by Les Ecologistes de l'Enzíève or Michael Lohman's *Guide complet de la Nature*. They can provide you with the right answers when one of the family asks what the large bird of prey soaring on a thermal high above your head is or what herbs and plants are producing the wonderful scents of the *garrigue* which they can smell. If you have children, then touring in this region could spark off in them a lifelong interest in nature.

In the spring the roadsides are covered in wild flowers. In the summer heat the ground becomes very dry and there is rather less to see, but by then the vines are rich in foliage and the grapes are appearing and many fields are full of sunflowers or poppies.

There are, however, some nasties, so be prepared. The mosquito for one! And lots of other flying insects in the woods and *garrigue* which will enjoy biting any bare flesh you are showing which hasn't been protected by an anti-insect gel or spray. There are just two creatures which in theory could give you a serious bite: scorpions and adders, but the chance of encountering either of them is fairly remote.

Starting with the coast, parts of it are designated as nature conservation areas and you will see signs to this effect but the degree of actual protection seems to vary a lot. See www.parc-naturelnarbonnaise.fr for details of walks in this area. The *Massif de la Clape* **Map F2** between Narbonne and the coast is an area of rugged lime-stone, about 17 km long by 8 km wide, much of it covered by *garrigue* where you can find a fine range of flowers, including several kinds of orchids and wild roses, and herbs such as rosemary and thyme.

Over half of it is a protected area. It is a good place for seeing birds – among them some uncommon ones such as Bonelli's eagles, short toed eagles and eagle owls. And it is an area rich in butterflies. When you are ready for some refreshment, remember that La Clape has its own *appellation* and is particularly noted for its fresh white wines – you can visit the *Chateau de l'Hospitalet* on the D168 to taste some of them.

The ***Etang de Pissevaches*** (and yes, the name does mean cow piss!) lies to the north of La Clape. It is a coastal lagoon with salt marshes which is a good area for bird watching especially at times of migration. The same is true of the lagoons around Gruissan. Between Gruissan and Port la Nouvelle you can visit the nature reserve of **Ile de Ste Lucie Map F3**. It has broad trails through its woods, see the above picture, ideal for walking or cycling. A narrow road from the edge of Port la Nouvelle which runs along part of the *Canal de la Robine* leads to the lock at the island where there is access to the marked trails.

Further south there is the lime-stone headland of Cap Leucate **Map F3** (see picture below) which is rich in flora in spring as well as being a good spot for watching migrant birds, best seen between March – May, and mid-August – October. Bob Gibbons in his 'Travellers' Nature Guide' to France describes what an exciting place this is for bird watching. He lists 'raptors such as honey buzzard, black kite, marsh harrier, short-toed eagle and a few ospreys'. Among the hundreds of

thousands of passing birds, he mentions 'finches, bee-eaters, red-rumped swallows, pipits including red-throated warblers, and shrikes' and among the birds breeding locally the 'blue rock thrush, speckled and orphean warblers, short-toed lark, black-eared wheatear, hoopoe and occasional great spotted cuckoos.'

To get to the headland there is a narrow road from the edge of Leucate Plage on the D649 up to the lighthouse on top of Cap Leucate but it is poorly sign-posted – just one little board saying 'Phare'.

Nearby are two lagoons, the **Etang de Leucate** and the **Etang de Lapalme Map E/F3** where flamingos, avocets and many other birds can be seen. It is reckoned that you can see some 200 species of birds and 700 species of plants along this stretch of the coast.

A drive in the summer sunshine through the Corbières hills especially where the road goes through the *garrigue* is a memorable experience not least because of the wonderful smells from the shrubs and wild herbs. In late summer you will find wild fig trees hanging rich with fruit and can see lizards flitting across the rocks and hear the rustling of cicadas.

If you love walking among trees Aude offers you plenty of choice from the extensive beech and chestnut forests at Loubatiere and Ramondens near **Le lac de Laprade Map C1** in the Montagne Noire to **La route du sapin**, the road through magnificent pine forests near Belcaire **Map B4** southwest of Limoux.

Carcassonne itself has an arboretum on **La colline de Pech Mary** – the Pech Mary hill to the south of the *Cité* which is at the heart of a listed site of 10 square km. In addition to trees native to the area there are some 50 other kinds which have been introduced. It will eventually become an eco-museum preserving local species as well as containing an area planted with over 20,000 fruit trees.

You can find arboretums in many places throughout the *département* – here are just a few of them. Near the village of Arques **Map C3** south of Quillan you can visit the **arboretum du Planel** which was started in 1933. It has majestic trees not native to the area such as Atlas cedars from Morocco, American red oaks, Sequoias, Virginian tulip trees and the ancient Gingko Biloba. A road leads up from the village to the Forest of Rialsesse.

At Seuil de Narouze **Map A1**, the watershed between the Atlantic and the Mediterranean, the arboretum there has an avenue of 61 plane trees planted at the beginning of the 19th century and

now more than 45 metres tall. Further north on the border of the *département*, more than 150 kinds of tree line the shores of the lake at Saint Ferréol **Map B1** with pathways through the woods.

One of the loveliest places to visit is the botanical garden, **La Bouichère Le Jardin aux Plantes**, on the edge of Limoux **Map C2** near the LeClerc and Bricomarche stores. It is a very extensive garden with some 2,500 varieties of plants, many of them rare. It exhibits in fact many different types of garden, e.g. a medieval one, a kitchen and medicinal herb garden, an English border garden, a tropical area, a fruit garden, a spice garden, a bamboo area, a recently created rose garden, a pond area and much more – all laid out in such a way that you can really enjoy them. Each tree and plant is identified by its Latin name and then by its French, English and German names. Benches are set in several shady areas, so you can sit and simply revel in all the colours, scents and beauty that surround you. There is a plant nursery and greenhouse with plants for sale.

La Bouichère is run by a very welcoming family who speak English. Admission is 5 € for adults, 2.50 € for older children but no charge for children under one metre high! Open June – August from 10.00 to 18.00 and May, Sept-Oct from 13.00 – 18.00 but it is closed on Mondays and Tuesdays. See www.labouichere.com

Some Wonders of Nature

France has some of the most beautiful underground sights in the world. You can find two of them just north of Carcassonne in the Montagne Noire. The **Grotte de Limousis** Map C1 is a wonderland of aragonite crystal formations, limestone curtains, scallop patterns on the ceiling, columns, stalagmites and stalactites and with some beautiful reflections in still pools. There is a 45 minute guided tour of the cave which stretches some 600 metres into the mountainside. The guides speak only French but a brief description in English printed on two sides of A4 paper is available from reception. Photography is permitted and there is a lot to photograph.

The tour ends in what is called the 'hall of chandeliers' the most spectacular of which hangs 4 metres down from the ceiling and has a circumference of 10 metres. It is truly majestic. And by an imaginative use of lighting which focuses in turn on the several formations of aragonite in that hall to the accompaniment of some appropriate music, it serves as a fitting finale to what is a magical experience underground. The cave is open in July and August from 10.30 to 18.00, during May, June and September there are guided tours at10.30/11.30/14.30/15.30/16.30 and 17.30 and during March and October just in the afternoons. In November it is open in the afternoon on Sundays and public holidays. Entry fee: 9€ for adults, reduced rates for school children. An added free bonus is a kilometre long path laid out up the hillside and planted with a variety of shrubs, herbs and trees native to the area – it takes about 15-20 minutes to walk and is accessible to all. A panoramic view of the lower countryside can be seen from the path.

Ten minutes drive away up the D112 through the *Gorges de la Clamoux* north of Villeneuve-Minervois is the **Gouffre de Cabrespine** Map C1, the deepest cavern in Europe and one of the deepest in the world. St Paul's Cathedral would fit in it very comfortably with space to spare. In fact you could fit two cathedrals in, one on top of the other! The route for visitors has been laid out in such a way that there are no steps, the paths simply slope down or up so it really is accessible for all. The view from the *balcon du Diable* is awe-inspiring – here is truly one of nature's wonders, the work of water on stone through millions of years leaving behind a myriad of beautiful stone and crystal formations. The standard tour lasts 45 minutes but for those with a special interest in caving and fit enough for it, it is possible to book a place on a five hour long exploration and much lower down led by a speliologist. The Cavern is open in July and August from 10.00 to 18.30; from April to June and in September from 10.00 to 12.00 and 14.00 to 18.00, in October 10.00 – 12.00 and 14.00 – 17.30; in March and November 14.00 - 17.30. Entry fee: 8€ for adults, 4€ for children. See www.grottes-de-france.com

Sticking with the effect of water on the landscape, there are some spectacular gorges to drive or walk through. The Michelin maps highlight the most scenic bits of any route by marking that stretch of the road green and there are plenty of them in the *département*.

The River Aude above Quillan has created a number of gorges where the mountains rise dramatically on both sides, sometimes for several hundred metres, for example at the **Défilé de la Pierre-Lys** Map C4. Near Axat is the **Gorges de St Georges** Map C4 where it narrows to about 20 - 25 metres with 300

metre high cliffs. Higher still up the River Aude, the D118 passes the *Grotte de l'Aguzou* **Map B4**. The cave is open to the public but can only be visited by appointment.

If you enjoy walking, Axat is a good centre as there are some fine walks towards Puilaurens and the Fenouillèdes in the east and towards the valley of the River Rebenty in the west. Heading east from Axat along the D117 and just over the border into the *département* of Roussillon is the *Gorges de Galumus* **Map C3** through which the River Agly flows. The road runs for some three km along a shelf which is carved out of the rock and frequently over-hangs the gorge. It is an exciting drive! You can park at the southern end where there is a good view down to what was once a small hermitage, the *Ermitage St Antoine de Galamus*. There is still a tiny chapel in a cave. The walk down to it takes about 15 minutes and is worth doing. The gorge is a lovely place for swimming and canyoning.

The *Massif de la Clape* south of Narbonne is a beautiful wild area of limestone outcrops and *garrigue* but also with a lot of vineyards on the lower slopes. One of its most striking natural features is *Le Gouffre de l'Œil Doux* **Map F2** pictured top right – the 'Sweet Eye Abyss' – a deep pool of fresh water yet so close to the sea.

On the D1118 about three miles north of St Pierre sur Mer there is a large, tree-shaded picnic area and car park which is the starting point for a 15 minute walk up a broad,

rocky path to the edge of the cliff overlooking the pool. It can also be reached from below if you fancy a swim in it.

A drive through the Corbières provides not only the experience of the garrigue with all its beautiful scents of wild herbs but also some wonderful views out over the landscape of vineyards. The stretch of road from Lagrasse to Tuchan past the Chateau d'Aguilar and on to Cucugnan and Queribus is exceptional **Map DE2/3 + ED3/2**.

There are fine views to be had from the roads leading up to the Montagne Noire and to Pic Nore and looking back down to the plain. Another is from the castle at Saissac **Map B1** down into the valley of the Vernessonne. These are just two of many.

There are thermal springs in the region which the Romans took advantage of to create spas. You can still enjoy the benefits of these naturally warm waters rich in minerals. Alet-les-Bains and Rennes-les-Bains **Map C3** are two such centres which have health and fitness programmes. At both places you can swim during the summer in an outdoor thermal pool. See www.renneslesbains.org

For the really high peaks and views from them you have to head to the southernmost part of the *département*, to the Pyrenees – to *Pic d'Ourthizat* at 1937 metres and *Pic de Madres* **Map C4** at 2469 metres. But before you reach them there are some exceptionally beautiful landscapes of high mountain pastures and thick forests which in spring display a wonderful array of shades of fresh green.

27

Music & Arts Festivals

All the events illustrated here from previous programmes are annual events. For the latest information about what's on culturally in the coming months in Carcassonne itself, look at the city's website where you will find a diary of events – www.carcassonne. org When you are down here the local daily paper *Midi Libre* has a column *Les Animations du Jour* which gives details of all concerts, plays, conferences, fairs, book signings, dances, lectures, children's activities etc that are on that day. You can be almost certain of finding something which would appeal to you. Two other sources of information for the wider region are www.tourisme-corbieres-miner-vois.com and www.aude-en-pyrenees.fr for details of what's on and where each month.

Carcassonne hosts a major arts and music festival in July each year with concerts at three different locations in the *Cité*. Only artists of national and international renown are invited to perform. The 2008 programme included concerts by Diana Ross, Deep Purple, George Benson, Massive Attack, ZZ Top, the National Orchestra of Lyons and many more. There are also ballet, opera and theatre performances. See the festival website for full details www.festivaldecarcassonne.com

July also sees *La Bastide festival* with some 70 free concerts in a variety of locations in the lower city. For details, see www.carcassonne-festivalde-labastide.com

There are other shorter festivals in Carcassonne throughout the year, for example, a **Jazz Week** in early April when five concerts are held in a recently restored former Jesuit College Chapel which has been specially fitted out for optimum acoustics. And a **Spanish Week** is held at the end of August when concerts and dance performances are given and there is opportunity to sample some Spanish gastro-nomic delights.

The magnificent organ in St Vincent's Church was completely renovated in 2006 and was then used for several concerts in an organ festival called *Les Vents d'Anges*. Two of the concerts were held in the Cathedral of Saint-Michel in the lower city. The former cathedral in the *Cité* has its own annual series of organ concerts, *Les Estivales d'Orgue de la Cité*.

In the winter and spring each year the *Chapelle des Jésuites* on *rue des Études* in the lower city is the venue for a series of classical orchestral concerts known as *Les Jeudis de l'Auditorium*. And at the beginning of April it hosts a Jazz Week – the 4 evening concerts cost just 40€ for all four.

You will also find concerts being held in abbeys, churches and castles out in the sticks. The

Saison musicale

Château de Rieux-Minervois

Château de Rieux-Minervois **Map D1** which is in the centre of that large village, hosts art exhibitions and concerts during the summer months. The concerts which are classical music are held once or twice a month on a Sunday afternoon at 17.00.

Caunes Minervois Map D1 also has a regular programme of concerts held in the abbey on Friday evenings at 21.30 followed by a wine tasting courtesy of one of the local vignerons. The series runs from early July to late August and includes classical concerts as well as popular contemporary music. Before each concert you can enjoy *une assiette gourmande* and drinks in the gardens of the abbey for 10€ but advance booking at the local tourist office is necessary for the meal. Each concert costs 15€ or all five concerts for 60€ – children under 16 are admitted free. See www.caunes-minervois.com

Béatrice and Graham Nutter host a summer season of concerts at their vineyard the ***Château Saint-***

Jacques d'Albas a couple of km from Laure Minervois **Map D1**. They have solo artists of international standing performing at them. See their website for details www.chateaustjacques.com. You can also sample some of their award winning wines.

The *Abbaye Ste-Marie d'Orbieu* in Lagrasse **Map D2** is used for concerts during the area's *Baroque en Minervois* series of concerts in June and for the *Fugue en Aude Romane* music festival in July. The other concerts in this series are held in abbeys and churches throughout Aude – at Caunes-Minervois, in the Abbey de Villelongue, St Hilaire, St Polycarpe, Alet-les-Bains and the church in Ouveillan. The website to check is www.fugueenauderomane.fr

The Abbey at **Fontfroide Map E2** is another venue for great performers. Their 2009 programme will include a *Festival Musique et Histoire* from 28th July to August 4th with concerts by Jordi Savall and Montserrat Figueras. See www.fontfroide.com for details.

The *Festival de Fontcalvy* **Map E1** is a mix of theatre, music and comedy held between mid-July and mid-August in a former Cistercian fortified barn near Ouveillan. The show begins at 22.00 but is preceded by a public, open-air meal at 19.30. See www.festival-fontcalvy.com

14 communes in the *Haute Vallée de l'Aude*, the upper reaches of the River Aude sponsor an International Festival of Folklore at the end of July and beginning of August each year. For details of these and other cultural events in this part of Aude, see www.aude-en-pyrenees.fr

Narbonne Map E2 has an arts festival called *Festa Latina* which runs from late June to the end of August and which celebrates the culture of the south through music, theatre, films, exhibitions, food and wine. Some of the events are held in Narbonne Plage. See the mairie's website for details – www.mairie-narbonne.fr

Jazz festivals are to be found throughout the region. One that has become an established annual event in the Montagne Noire is *Jazz sous les châtaigniers* – Jazz under the chestnut trees. It is held in early August at the *château de Roquefère* near the famous cavern at Limoussis. For more details, see www.jazz-roquefere.com

There is no shortage of music making in Aude, especially in the summer. Expect to find concerts all over the place, even in quite small villages such as Pennautier **Map C2** which hosts a *Festival International de Piano* in mid August.

Lots of villages have a *Fête de la Musique* on 21 June when amateur as well as professional musicians bring music to the streets.

An art festival started in 2002 in the Upper Valley of the Aude which has grown and become an annual event is the *Chemin des Artistes* which takes place from 21st – 24th May. It involves some 50 artists in 20 different communes of the Haute-Vallée de l'Aude. The programme includes concerts, lectures, films, guided forest and upland walks for bird watching as well as art exhibitions. Half a dozen of the communes offer a *Repas Champêtre* at lunch time each day for between 8 and 12 €.

The artists welcome visitors to their studios not just during this festival but throughout the year. The poster pictured below was designed by Ellie Clemens, an American artist who has exhibited her work at this festival in the past. For more details, see www.chemindesartistes.com

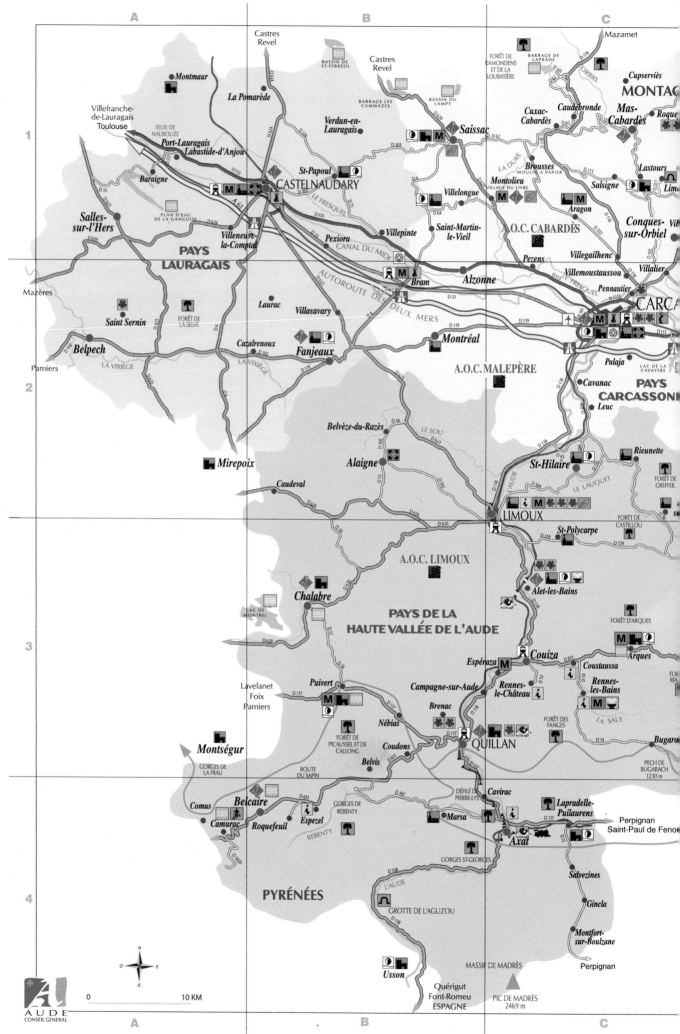

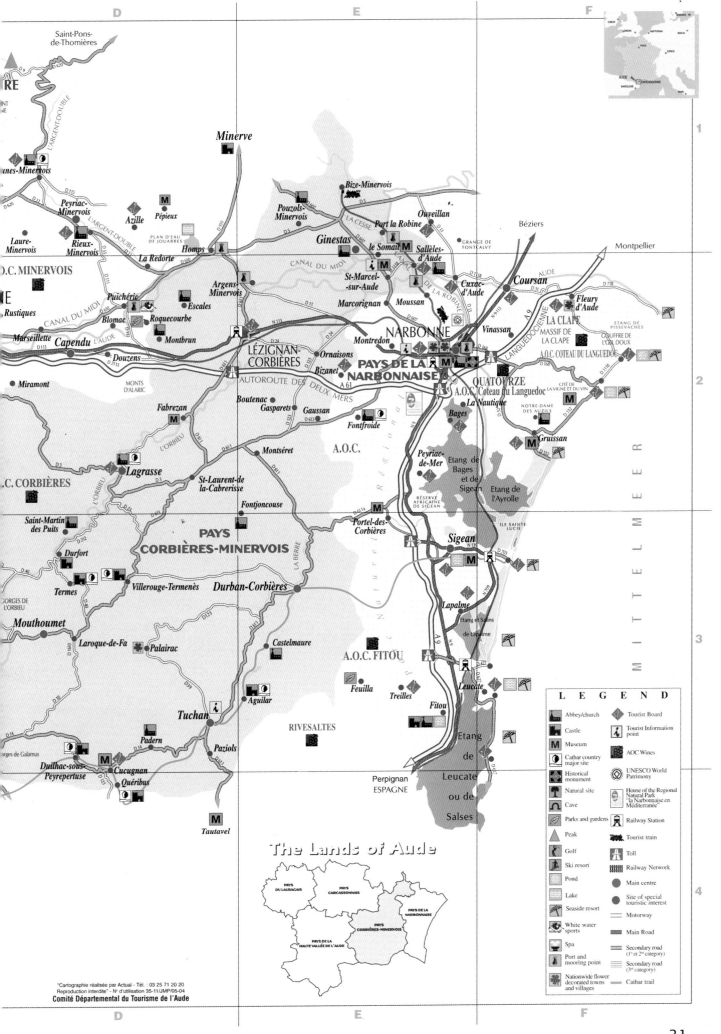

The Lands of Aude

LEGEND

Abbey/church		Tourist Board
Castle		Tourist Information point
Museum		AOC Wines
Cathar country major site		UNESCO World Patrimony
Historical monument		House of the Regional Natural Park "la Narbonnaise en Méditerranée"
Natural site		Railway Station
Cave		Tourist train
Parks and gardens		Toll
Peak		Railway Network
Golf		Main centre
Ski resort		Site of special touristic interest
Pond		Motorway
Lake		Main Road
Seaside resort		Secondary road (1er et 2nd category)
White water sports		Secondary road (3rd category)
Spa		Cathar trail
Port and mooring point		
Nationwide flower decorated towns and villages		

"Cartographie réalisée par Actual - Tél. : 03 25 71 20 20
Reproduction interdite" - N° d'utilisation 35-11/JMP/05-04
Comité Départemental du Tourisme de l'Aude

Shopping

Les Délices de Terroir is a sign you will often see in villages and occasionally at some of the sites you visit. It indicates that good quality local products are on sale there, usually foodstuffs of many kinds as well as wines, liqueurs, and confectionery such as nougat and pralines. There is a good choice of bottled or canned regional produce which will provide savoury memories of your holiday: stuffed olives, anchovies, foie gras, cassoulet, honey, olive products, and caramelised nuts.

All the really big stores are to be found in the commercial areas on the edge of town. The French supermarket chains: *Géant*, *LeClerc*, and *Intermarché* are all situated there. *Géant* has two branches, one on the *Z.I. La Bouriette* near the airport and the A9 motorway junction nr 23, the other on a small industrial estate off the D6113 heading out of town towards Narbonne. *LeClerc* is on the northern bypass as you head out to the airport. They can't be missed as they all have enormous signs advertising their presence! *Intermarché* is on a small estate called *Z.I.Pont Rouge* on the road heading north in the direction of Mazamet. If you are touring by car, it is in your interests to find them as petrol and diesel are significantly cheaper there than anywhere else. In fact just about everything is cheaper there, food, wine, clothes, electrical goods etc. The *zones industrielles et commercielles* are home to lots of other big stores selling home furnishings, D.I.Y., shoes, lighting, toys, and much else.

Unlike Britain, French shops do not have so-called 'Sales' (*Soldes* in French) on most of the time. There are just two fixed sales seasons a year, each one lasting five weeks. In 2009 the starting dates are the second Wednesday in January and the last Wednesday in June. Shops are also allowed to choose two further weeks but these short *soldes flottantes* must end at least a month before the start of the fixed ones. You can pick up some real bargains, both in specialist shops and in the supermarkets. You will, however, often see goods marked down in price at other times or special offers even if it isn't an official sales week. Opening

hours for shops are usually 10.00 – 19.00 though some open at 09.00, and supermarkets are usually 09.00 – 20.00. Shops are not normally open on Sundays.

Honey comes in many flavours and a variety of forms, so why not visit one of the places that specializes in this natural product? One km outside the village of Montseret at Hameaux des Clauses **Map E2** on the D423 there is a beekeepers co-operative which welcomes visitors. It is called *Miellerie des Clauses*.

One of the beekeepers will be happy to talk about their work and answer questions, and one of the staff speaks English. On show is a transparent hive so you can see the bees at work inside. You can taste honey in a variety of flavours – acacia, flowers of the garrigue, rosemary, and many more, or sample a small glass of mead along with a piece of honey cake, or buy some honey soap! It is only a small place but worth a visit. Look out for the yellow signs along the road to it. It is open every day from 08.00 – 12 and from 14.00 – 18.00, and you can take part in an hour long free guided tour. See www.miellerie-des-clauses.com

One speciality shop that chocoholics will want to patronise is the *Chocolatier*. France has some of the world's finest chocolate

makers. It is a highly skilled profession and their products are truly scrumptious. There is a chocolatier in Carcassonne on the *Place Carnot* and in the *Cité* you will also find a specialist sweet shop – *La Cure Gourmande*. If you are touring in the upper valley of the Aude, there is an excellent *chocolatier* at Luc sur Aude near Couiza **Map C3** called *Nougalet* and another award winning one in Quillan, *Confiserie LUMEL*.

Another sweet product made in villages of the Montagne Noire are *Carbardises* delicious caramelised walnuts, hazelnuts and almonds – definitely 'more-ish' for nut lovers. The *Pralinerie du Mazet* in Brousses-et-Villaret **Map C1** has won awards for theirs.

Still on the subject of food, the French love their bread – a meal is lacking if there is no bread on the table. Many villages still have their own *boulangeries*, bakeries

selling fresh bread in many shapes and sizes, *ficelles, baguettes longues* or *court, flutes, pain de campagne* or flavoured in some particular way such as *pain au noix*. Newly baked bread is available early morning, noon and evening. There are also several kinds of *brioche* and *viennoiserie*, sweet soft bread, as well as a range of delicious cakes and pastries such as the large, flaky *oreillettes* or huge, crumbly meringues.

Another shop for those who enjoy their food is the **traiteur** or delicatessen where you can buy ready made meals prepared on the premises. In addition to the specialist shops of this kind in town centres, you will find such departments in the bigger supermarkets too. The food is reasonably priced and the quality is generally very good.

There are few departmental stores in town centres, **Monoprix** is the exception in Carcassonne but there is no shortage of specialist shops: clothes boutiques, lingerie, hats, leather goods, shoes, jewellery, perfumes, soft furnishings, toys, mobile phones, etc. Bookshops are called **Librairies**, and English newspapers (a day late) are usually available wherever you see the word **Presse** above the shop. You can find a cheap selection of second hand English paperbacks in the English Shop on *rue Armagnac* near St Vincent's Church – the shop specializes in British food.

Brocante means second hand goods, furniture in particular, and you will occasionally see the sign out in villages as well as in towns. Carcassonne has a sale of this kind once a month at the *André Chénier* Gardens near the port – see the poster on the right. Narbonne has a similar sale every Sunday morning along the banks of the canal in the town centre.

Vide grenier, car boot sales, are advertised on flyers you will see stuck in shop windows and are usually to be found in villages and held on Sundays. You will also see a single stall in car laybys selling whatever is in season on their bit of land: fresh asparagus, peaches, melons. Or sometimes it is a fish farmer come up from the coast with his harvest of **coquillages** mussels and other shell fish.

Mention has already been made of the fruit and vegetable markets on *Place de Carnot* in Carcassonne. You will also find a good range of other specialist food products there such as Catalan sausages, cheeses and all kinds of marinated olives. There is also a very large cheap clothes market along the *Boulevard Barbès* on Tuesday, Thursday and Saturday mornings.

The Romans introduced the olive tree to the region and olive oil is still an important constituent of local cooking. The only olive cooperative in Aude is the **Coopérative l'Oulibo** at *Bize Minervois* **Map E1** founded in 1942. The olives grown here are called *Lucque de Bize* and are regarded by connoisseurs as being among

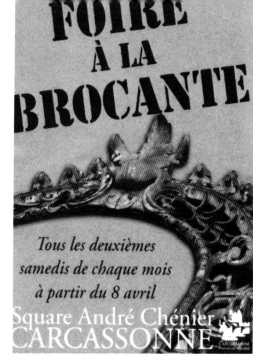

the best. You can taste them, prepared in different ways, at their shop. It also has a good range of other local products: honey, goat's cheese, cooked meats, nougat, wines and brandies, as well as items made from olive tree wood. It is open throughout the year from 08.00 – 12 and 14.00 –19.00 with free guided tours from 10.30 – 17.30 in the summer. See www.loulibo.com

Among the souvenirs that you decide to take back home, do include some bottles of local wine and preferably bought direct from vineyards you have visited. The wine industry in France is going through a very hard time at present largely because national consumption has fallen and because New World wines are better marketed. The more you buy, the greater the help you will be giving to the local economy.

Arts and Crafts

If you have time for just one craft shop, then make it *la Coopérative Artisanale du "Vieux Lavoir"* on *rue du Plo* in Carcassonne's *Cité*. Here you will find an excellent selection of beautiful goods hand-made by craftsmen in the region – pottery, leather, glass, metal, linen, silk, paintings and much else. It is a real treasure trove of a place. It has information leaflets about several of those who have made the goods. Details are given of where their workshops are to be found should you want to pay them a visit to see more of their work or even perhaps to commission a particular piece as a special gift.

Some of the tourist sites that attract lots of visitors such as particular castles or abbeys have art and crafts exhibitions during the summer months – the *Château d'Arques* Map C3, for example, pictured above has exhibitions of particular painters a fortnight at a time from the end of May through to the end of August.

A few miles to the south of Arques in the hamlet of St Louis et Parahou, Jonathan Moss has his *Atelier St Louis*. He is a well established British painter whose work is inspired by the beauty of the region. He writes of this on his website – "I am consumed by awe at the stillness and sometimes overpowering force of nature, which acts as a means to reveal an internal landscape." Read and see more at www.atelierstlouis.com

He is an artist truly worth meeting.

The *Abbaye de Villelongue* Map B1 is host to an exhibition of *sculptures dans les jardins* from April to October and during the summer it has an art exhibition in the refectory (see right). The village of Montolieu has art and photographic and sculpture exhibitions at *La Coopérative*, its *Centre d'Art et de Littérature*.

Many of the small towns and villages you may pass through as you tour the region will have signs indicating that *artisans*, craftsmen, are based there – potters are the most usual – and often you can watch them at work. The word to look out for is *poterie*. Dominique Devouard is one of them whose workshop and showroom is open throughout the year from 10.00 – 12 apart from Sunday mornings and from 15.00 – 20.00. You can find her at *Poterie des Pontils* on the *Route d'Arques* at Peyrolles Map C3. The well stocked shop there also sells pottery by other craftsmen.

Another pottery is that of Lionel Postal at the northern end of Caunes Minervois Map D1. The town also has a painter's and sculptor's studio (Jean Michel Lafite) and a marble workshop. Caunes, naturally, has its own Festival of Marble Sculpture which in 2009 will be held in front of the Abbey on 7 June. See www.lesmarbrieresdecaunes.fr

If you are travelling along the *Canal du Midi* and reach the *ecluse d'Aiguilles* near Puichéric the lock keeper, Joël Barthes, is a wood carver and exhibits his work there.

On the D168, the road from Narbonne to Narbonne Plage, which runs through La Clape peninsula Map F2 you pass the

Château de l'Hospitalet which is now a luxurious hotel owned by Gérard Bertrand, a former Narbonne

rugby star. It also houses a variety of art and craft workshops as well as a wine centre, a museum of historical curios and an art gallery. There is a programme of international art exhibitions which changes every second month, and in the summer there is a festival of classical music and a jazz festival held in the castle courtyard. And, as you might expect, a *restaurant gastronomique* and a *bistrot*. See www.gerard-bertrand.com

Mention has already been made of the **European Patchwork Centre** in Sallèles d'Aude (see page 23). Exhibitions of work by national and international artists in materials are shown throughout the year and it is sometimes possible to buy the exhibits. Some of them command high prices but they are unique pieces created by great craftswomen.

The small town of Lagrasse
Map D2 is labelled a *Ville et Métiers d'Art* because of the large number of artisans with workshops there: craftsmen in wood, leather, metal, ceramics, stained glass, jewellery, and designers of clothes and furniture. The neighbouring village of Mayronnes has an annual Sculpture Walk *Sentier Sculpturel* which is open from April to September.

The village of Minerve **Map E1** is another spot for potters, and artists where you can buy some beautiful mementos of your visit. The children pictured above are admiring the craft work on display in a shop in Minerve.

If you are touring north of Carcassonne and passing through Cuxac Cabardés, stop at Daniel Haran's studio at 21 *route de Mazamet*. He sculpts in wood and stone, and accepts commissions to do busts based on photographs of the subject.

You will often find artists, potters and sculptors displaying their work at the autumn wine festivals in the towns and villages all over the region. Sometimes you can see several of them at work in the same place. At the Caunes marble festival, for example, you can watch sculptors in ice as well as marble and workers of wrought iron. Quite a mix and not to be missed.

Eating out

Food is taken seriously in France and is a frequent topic of conversation! Shopkeepers are usually ready to advise on how to prepare and cook what you have bought from them. I remember the first time I bought asparagus from a stallholder in Carcassonne market, seeing that I was not French he immediately volunteered information on how best to prepare the vegetable he had grown. And when my wife first bought some slices of home cured ham in our village shop which the shopkeeper had just cut for her, he insisted that she took a melon to go with it which he chose for her – he wanted us to enjoy our lunch in the way he would.

Cafés, brasseries and restaurants always display their menus outside the building so that you can see what is on offer and what it will cost you. There will often be three or four *Menu Fixe or Formules* at various levels and prices. It is always cheaper to eat at lunch time when a simple menu of *entrée, plat du jour*, and *dessert* or coffee is on offer. Few places have menus in English though some do, so it is worth asking. Here are some of the dishes you might see listed:

Entrées:
Soupe de l'oignon – onion soup,
soupe de poissons – fish soup,
potage aux légumes – vegetable soup.
pâté de foie gras – goose liver pâté,
pâté maison – home made pâté, usually of pork.

When melons are in season, they figure as an *entrée*, served either with cured ham or filled with sweet Muscat wine or with port. Two other common options are:

Cruditées – a plate of chopped raw vegetables – and *charcuterie*: a plate of sliced cooked meats. Bread is always served but without butter. It is customary in France to wait till your meal arrives before tucking into the bread!

Salades: Sometimes the salad simply has a name, e.g. *salade composée, salade Nicoise* or *salade Cathare* and you will have to ask the waiter what is in it but often the menu will list all the main ingredients, lettuce, beans, onions, tomatoes, eggs, and anchovies, or whatever. A French salad is usually a substantial plateful – almost a meal in itself.

Pizzas: these usually list the ingredients e.g. *trois fromages* might have the three cheeses: *chevre, cantal* and *roquefort*.

Viandes or **Grillades**: you will be asked how you want your meat cooked:
bleu very rare –
saignant(e) rare –
à point/rose medium
or *bien cuit* well-done.

Most meat dishes come with potatoes, usually *frites* but also *sautées* or *dauphine*.
Steak hachée is a minced beef burger and figures regularly on children's menus but it will not be well done unless you request it. A 'fast food' dish which occasionally appears on children's menus is *saucisse de Toulouse avec frites*, which is a bit like Cumberland sausage with chips.

Top of the local meat specialities is the white bean stew cassoulet using the Castelnaudary recipe which has pieces of shoulder of pork, sausage and preserved duck or simply with duck though many restaurants have their own variation of this favourite and substantial dish. A similar one is *Fricassée de Limoux* made from white beans and with ham. Sirloin steaks figure on many menus and come with a variety of sauces, *entrecôte au poivre* and *entrecôte au Roquefort* being two of them. *Magret de canard*, breast of duck is another regular dish.

More special regional dishes include – *Panaché d'agneau à la fleur de thym du Cabardès et clafoutis de legumes* which is a lamb dish from the area north of Carcassonne. From the Minervois area's cuisine, there is *civet de sanglier* a stew of boar's meat preferably served with a good full bodied red wine from the Corbières or the Minervois and for dessert *Figuettes des Corbières*, a fig tart served with almond cream. From Narbonne's culinary heritage *Poêlée de coquillages aux pignons de pin* a pan of shellfish dressed in pine kernels. Tripe and horse meat will often be found on menus.

Omelettes of many kinds are available – a rather special Audoise dish is *omelette d'asperges sauvages* – made with local wild asparagus.

Desserts: *iles flottantes* – squares of marshmallow in custard *crème caramel* or *crème catalan mousse au chocolat*

various tartes e.g. *tarte aux pommes* – apple pie
Mouilleux is a rich, soft chocolate cake

There is usually a separate ice cream menu (not cheap) or cheese may be offered as an alternative to a dessert in a fixed price menu. More expensive *menus fixes* will include a cheese course which usually consists of two or three small pieces of local cheeses.

Coffee is extra and unless otherwise requested will come in a tiny cup. If you are wanting milky coffee, ask for *un grand café crème*. You may also be asked if you would like a *digestif* such as cognac or a local brandy.

The house wine served in a ¼, ½ or 1 litre jug called a *pichet* is usually a drinkable cheap local red, rosé or white wine. Occasionally even with this cheap option, the grapes used to make the wine will be listed.

The bill is *l'addition*. The service charge and taxes are almost always included (TTC), but doesn't attentive service deserve a few extra euros?

Take time over your meal! The lunch break lasts two hours 12.00-14.00. Expect to spend longer in the evening when the meal will be more expensive. Dinner isn't usually served much before 19.30, and it is worth reserving a table if you are planning to go to one of the better and more popular restaurants.

The Aude Tourist Board has produced a very attractive, free 28 page booklet **Gastronomie & Vins**

which gives recipes for regional dishes with information about suitable wines to be drunk with them; it also includes a list of recommended restaurants with details of opening hours and price range. In addition to the many bars and brasseries serving tasty food, there are some fine restaurants which serve regional dishes but few can match the setting of *La Rôtisserie* in the castle at Villerouge **Map D3**. Here you can dine as though you were a 14th century noble – for details see www.restaurant-medieval.com

Another one in a rather special setting, a renovated 18th century stable, which is one of my own favourites in Carcassonne is *L'écurie* at 43 Boulevard Barbès – see www.restaurantlecurie.fr

The village of Brugairolles is up the Aude valley in the direction of Limoux where you will find the Domaine Gayda with a gourmet restaurant – it serves good food in a lovely setting. See www.domainegayda. com

Night life

Most tourists don't come to Carcassonne or to the region for its night life but if you do want to go clubbing and dance the night away there are plenty of venues where you can do this.

The free entertainment provided in the summer in the beach resorts includes lots of open air concerts and dances. The newspaper *L'Indépendent* has an inset (*Le Journal de l'été*) every day during July and August listing everything that is going on in the region including all the live music events.

Many restaurants and bars stay open till about midnight. After that it is over to the night spots, the *bars de nuit*, some of which stay open at weekends until five next morning.

Carcassonne has a number of Latino bars and clubs, among them *La Fiesta Bodega* at 49 *avenue Dr Henri Goût* open Wednesdays to Saturdays from 19.00 to five next morning. Another is the *Haberna Café* at 23 *place Carnot* **Town Map B2**. *Le Makhila* at 15 *Bd de Varsovie* **Town Map A1** is a Basque bar open every day from 06.30 – 02.00 which serves excellent *tapas*. *Bar Le 98* at 12 *rue Georges Clémenceau* **Town Map B2** is a traditional bar with music and the occasional special theme evening, open until two in the morning at weekends.

Just a street away from the main square at 16 *rue de l'Aigle d'Or* is *Le Conti* which describes itself as the only true *bar musical* in the centre of town. It is more than that as it hosts all kinds of

entertainment: fashion shows and theme nights as well as live concerts. It is reckoned to be one of the liveliest night spots in town. It is open from 18.00 – 02.00 Thursday – Saturday, and from 22.00 on other evenings.

The *Café de Nuit* at 31 *Boulevard Omer Sarraut* **Town Map B1** attracts a mixed gay/straight clientele – but note it has an age restriction for entry: over 25 and under 50.

La Bulle at the foot of the *Cité* at 115 *rue de Barbacane* **Town Map C3** is a dance club with a restaurant. The club is described in one French guide as having an '*ambience torride garanti!*', so be warned! It is closed Mondays and Tuesdays. There is no entry charge but they reserve the right to refuse entry, as do some other clubs.

A Karaoke bar not far from the town centre is *L'eclipse* at 30 *rue Minervoise* which runs alongside the *Canal du Midi* **Town Map C1**.

For those who want to drink Irish beer and whiskey and listen to

live music there is *O'Sheridan's Pub* at 13 *rue Victor Hugo* **Town Map B2**. Another Irish bar is *The Celt* at 5 *rue Armagnac* just a few yards from *Place Carnot*.

Further out on the edge of town is the *Black Bottom discotheque* on the *Route de Limoux*. And on the D6113 – the *Route de Trèbes* is *Le Rockadélic* which usually has a rock concert on a Friday night starting at 21.00. And on the *Route de Mazamet* is *Le Living Room*.

A new club for those aged over 27 is *Le Souvenir* which is on the shopping and industrial estate called *Zi La Bouriette* near the airport on the western edge of town. This is a big estate but look for the big store called *Decathlon* as the club is opposite it. It is open only on Fridays and Saturdays from 22.00 – they list the music they play there as being 'disco, dance, 80's, house, French, pop-rock, slow, ambiance, zouk and techno.'

The monthly information leaflet *Agenda des Loisirs* lists several more bars which have DJs or where you can hear live music. And the free bi-monthly culture magazine *Le Mag* gives details of upcoming concerts. You can pick up copies of these publications from the main tourist office in Carcassonne.

Narbonne which is the largest town in Aude also has its night spots. Among them are two discotheques, *Sappho* and *Anthineus*, at the same address – 39 *avenue de Bordeaux* – which attract large numbers of young people, gay as well as straight. Another dance club is *Le Talgo* at 8 *avenue des Pyrénées*. The *Why Not Café* and *Le Bal Masqué* at 4 and 6 *rue Marcelin-Coural* both have live bands and DJs.

The *Chakana Club* on the *avenue de Forum* on the industrial estate *Zi Croix-Sud* is a discotheque which has some well known DJs.

It claims to be a paradise for lovers of electro music. It is open Thursdays to Sundays. See its website www.chakana-club.fr

Other *bars de nuits* in Narbonne, all open until 02.00 are *Le Botafogo* and *Le Zanzibar* on *avenue des Pyrénées*, and *Le Fair Play* at 9 *boulevard du Général de Gaulle*. The last two attract mostly the young crowd in their 20s.

The city's *Festa Latina* which runs from mid-June to August provides some great opportunities to listen to Latin music and to dance the salsa, mambo, cha-cha-cha and tango. Bands play on a barge, the *peniche d'Oc*, moored in the *Canal de la Robine*. Free tuition is given in the salsa at the *Place de Forum* on Mondays from 18.30.

A beach discotheque with a difference is the *Lydia*, pictured below. It is a large white liner on

the beach at Port-Bacarès just south of Port-Leucate. The *Lydia* also serves as a restaurant and casino. It closed temporarily at the end of 2008 but the owners said it would re-open for the 2009 summer holiday season.

Gruissan too has a casino, *Le Phoebus*, on the *Boulevard de la Sagne*. It includes a karaoke pub. As with all casinos there is a minimum age of 18 for playing certain games. See www.phoebus-sa.com

Another casino-cum-restaurant, pictured above, is in the upper valley of the river Aude on the main road near Alet-les-Bains. It is open from 11.00 to four next morning and has live music on Friday and Saturday nights.

I have mentioned a few bars which are reputed to be favoured by gays. The gay scene in Aude does not have a high profile. Most people have a relaxed attitude to sexual orientation which is regarded as a private matter and therefore not something to publicise. If you want to meet socially with local gays then a good first move could be to ring the gay network number in Montpellier 08 92 39 04 34. Websites which might be useful are www.gaipied.fr www.gayguide.net/Europe/France and www.gayvox.com

For more general information about the gay scene in France, you can check out the *Petit Futé* annual guide published each March called *France Gay & Lesbien*.

Towns and Villages of Interest

The large town of **Castelnaudary Map B1** is to the west of Carcassonne on the D613. It has been the capital of the Lauragais since the 15th century and is best known for being the home of the regional dish *cassoulet*. There are plenty of restaurants and other food outlets in the town where you can buy it. Half-day *cassoulet* cookery courses are held in the autumn. Whilst the older part of the town does not compare with the *Cité* it does have some lovely old buildings, notably the *Presidial*, once a courthouse and prison, with its beautiful Renaissance frontage built on the orders of Catherine de Medici, Queen of France and Countess of the Lauragais. There are also a number of 17th and 18th century private mansions nearby and the parish church, *l'église St-Michel*, which has some interesting modern (as well as ancient) pieces of sculpture, e.g. two polychrome wooden carvings of the Resurrection and of Our Lady of Lourdes. Follow the directions for the centre of town and park near the large and striking War Memorial. The steps behind it lead up to the *Palais de Justice* which has an attractive play area for children in front of it, and nearby is the oldest part of the town. Castelnaudary was once an important commercial port on the *Canal du Midi* but its *Grand Bassin* is now home just to pleasure boats.
See www.ville-castelnaudary.fr

Mirepoix Map A2 is situated just outside Aude in the Ariège but is such a delightful place and so near, it has to be included. Head for the ancient part of the town, a typical *bastide*, where there is plenty of parking near the medieval cathedral which is worth a look inside. The town is most famous for the wooden arcades around the square, pictured below, which adjoins the cathedral and for the very many fine carvings on the beam ends jutting out above the arcades, mostly dating from the 12th and 13th centuries. You will find some good shops and cafés here. The town hosts many events which attract large numbers of visitors, among them an antiques fair and puppet festival and in late July a medieval tournament – **les Médiévales de Mirepoix** which includes a concert and a ball.
See www.ot-mirepoix.fr

Limoux Map C2 is another attractive large town situated to the south of Carcassonne on the route to the Pyrenees. The tourist office is on the main road the D118 and there is free parking across the road from it. A short walk takes you down into the town centre where you will find a pretty square with arcades round it – see above. It is here that the revellers parade and sing and dance at weekends during what must be the world's longest carnival – it lasts from January till a fortnight before Easter and has been an annual event since the Middle Ages. Driving into town you cannot mistake what is its biggest export: the original French sparkling wine *Blanquette de Limoux* and a stop for sampling some is a must for any visitor. Limoux is also known for its fine nougat and for the local dish *fricassée de Limoux*, a pork and bean stew not unlike *cassoulet*. There are some medieval remains notably the parish church of St Martin and parts of the 14th century town walls. The tourist office on the *Promenade du Tivoli* is at the same location as the *Musée Petiet* which has a beautiful collection of French paintings from *la belle Époque*. On *Place du 22 Septembre* in the *Eglise St Jacques* is France's only museum devoted solely to pianos and their manufacture – it has about 60 of them but it is only open for a limited period in the summer. A new attraction in 2009 is a small tourist train which does a 40 minute circuit of the best sights in town – it costs 5€ for adults and 3€ for children. See www.limoux.fr

A much visited small village on top of a hill in the upper valley of the Aude is **Rennes-le-Chateau Map C3** – see www.rennes-le-chateau.fr – which would probably never have figured on any tourist's itinerary had it not been for the book *The Holy Blood and the Holy Grail*. Unless you are hooked on the story, it is not really worth the detour. The spa town of **Alet-les-Bains** nearby is much more interesting with more to offer. As has **Rennes-les-Bains** with its thermal baths (five hot springs and four cold ones) and its open air thermal pool. See www.renneslesbains.org for more details of the spa treatment on offer.

Caunes Minervois Map D1 was a fortified town in the Middle Ages and has retained a number of houses from the 14th-17th centuries but its chief attraction is its abbey church founded in 791 and the related monastic buildings which the town council has been renovating in recent years (see page 11). There is a large car park with a children's play area next to it near the *Mairie* and it is just a short walk from there to the abbey. There is a potter's workshop at the top end of the town (literally up the hill). A kilometre away are some of the old marble quarries and there is a pleasant walk along a good path to them. See www.caunes-minervois.fr

Between Caunes and Narbonne and just over the border in the *département* of Herault is the pretty village of Minerve **Map E1** – now listed as one of *les plus beaux villages de France*. The village was made famous by the slaughter of 140 Cathars there on 22nd July 1210. It was the first mass burning of prisoners taken in the crusade against them. The village had the natural protection of being sited on a rocky spur dominating the gorges of the rivers *La Cesse* and *Brian* but it fell when access to its water supply was cut off by the pounding of de Montfort's heavy artillery. Parking is outside the village which you enter via a bridge over the gorge.

Lagrasse Map D2 too is counted among the most beautiful villages in France. It has a lovely setting on the river Orbieu. In addition to its famous abbey (see page 11) founded by Charlemagne it is rich in medieval buildings. The market place pictured below is especially fine. And it has some good craft shops and restaurants. Definitely worth a stop when you are driving through the Corbières.

Montolieu Map C1 is the French equivalent of Hay on Wye – a town of second hand bookshops. But it is a pretty village too set on a rock outcrop between two steeply sloping gorges and surrounded by vineyards and *garrigue* on which about 60 *Capitelles Montolivaines* are still to be seen – the small dry stone huts which were once used by shepherds and vineyard workers. The village has a 14th century church built in late Gothic style set on the square where there is a good restaurant, appropriately named *La Marque Page*. Given what it is now famous for – books – there are quite a few literary events in the course of each year. The Michel Braibant Museum which is about the history of writing and printing is worth a visit, and usually also has a good art exhibition on upstairs. See www.montolieu.fr

Narbonne Map E2 is the largest town in the *département* with a history as old as that of Carcassonne. The Romans made it one of their major cities on the road to Spain and it quickly became famous for its wine exports. You can still see a small part of the *via Domitia* in the square near the Cathedral, and the underground storage rooms of that era, the *horraeum*, can be visited. The *Musée Lapidaire* houses an extensive collection of Roman remains – one of the best in Europe. In the early Middle Ages the Archbishops of Narbonne were powerful figures and took a leading role in persecuting the Cathars. Their cathedral begun in 1272 was intended to be the largest in France and a symbol of the Catholic Church's power but only the chancel was completed. Their former residence, the *Palais des Archeveques*, next door to the cathedral is open to visitors. Its cloisters have some striking gargoyles – see above – and it has a fine archaeological museum. The town has its own canal, the *Canal de la Robine*, which links up with the *Canal du Midi*. And a tourist train runs from the railway station down to Port la Nouvelle stopping at the nature reserve at *Ile de Ste Lucie* en route. There are lots of good shops, an extensive market on both banks of the canal, and many eating places – one of the best is the *Bistrot du Chef en Gare*. The town boasts an Olympic size outdoor swimming pool heated to 27°c at the *Espace de Liberté* see www.espaceliberte.com Other amenities on the same site include indoor pools, an ice rink, bowling and a skate park plus a restaurant with a simple but mouth-watering menu: an eat as much as you want buffet. The town has a lot going for it but street parking in the centre can prove difficult and a few more signposts there indicating how to get out of town are needed. A centrally located underground car park is *Les Halles - Mirabeau*. It is right by the canal market, just five minutes walk from the Archbishop's Palace and other cultural sights, and if you fancy exploring just a few kilometres of the canal, you can hire a small electrically powered boat close to where you exit the car park. Alternatively, between 10th April and 15th October, you can take a 40 minute ride on *le petit train de Narbonne* which drives round the main sights in town. For more information see www.mairie-narbonne.fr

Touring in the Region

There is no shortage of hotel accommodation but the chains of cheap ones such as Etap and Formule 1 will usually only be found on the outskirts of the larger towns. Carcassonne and Narbonne have the full range from cheap hostels to five star. Elsewhere you will find modest one or two star hotels, and occasionally more luxurious but expensive ones sometimes in converted *châteaux*. In the villages you are more likely to find small inns, *auberges*, or *gîtes* belonging to villagers or *chambres d'hôtes* where eating with your hosts may be an option. The main website for *gîtes* is www.gites-de-france-aude.com   More information about accommodation is on pages 55-56.

However limited your knowledge of spoken French may be, don't be afraid to try it out. Many owners do not speak English or very little, and they will be very pleased if you make the effort to speak their language.

Many farms now do B + B and/or have *gîtes* or have a permit and all the necessary washing and toilet facilities for camping on their land. Farms are normally limited to just 25 pitches for tents or caravans, so you can be fairly sure it will be quiet and peaceful. A few of them also offer an evening meal and at many more you can buy fresh produce grown or made on the farm. The Aude Chamber of Agriculture has published an attractive and informative booklet entitled **Bienvenue à la ferme dans l'Aude**,

'Welcome to the Farm', which gives full details. Copies are available from tourist offices. They also have a website at www.bienvenue-a-la-ferme.com

Driving along you will often see signs for *chambres d'hôtes* and occasionally at vineyards which will give you the added bonus if you stay there of discovering first hand something of the science of wine making. Many of the *chambres d'hôtes* are checked and commended for quality by the regional board. You will see a sign indicating what their rating is.

Ex-pats too are now doing this as it is one of the few means of being self-employed and making a living open to them. Many have their own websites. If you are toying with the idea of moving to the region, you might find it helpful to stay with an ex-pat family who can tell you how they have coped with the move and the change of culture and they can explain something of the formalities and requirements which are inevitably a part of relocating to a new country.

The Tourist Office has leaflets and booklets about routes tourists may wish to follow – wine routes in particular. Also popular is **la Route des Cathares** which takes you to all the castles and sites related to the Cathars and the Catholic Church's crusade against them in the 13th century. The website www.tourisme-corbieres- miner-vois.com suggests a variety of car trails. If you are planning to visit the Upper valley of the Aude, www.payshva.org is a good source of information.

The Tourist Office in Carcassonne also organizes a couple of bus tours, the one visits sites in the Corbières and the other in the Cabardès area. On pages 49 –53 you will find 8 routes I have devised which include many of the sites recommended in this guide.

Be sure to have a full tank of petrol or diesel if you are heading off into the countryside. There is an absence of petrol stations out in the sticks! It is easy to

get caught out. Driving along winding, hilly roads and in low gear uses more petrol than you think.

In addition to the normal road signs used all over the EU, many French towns and villages have created their own for reminding drivers to slow down and drive carefully through their village – see the one pictured below which you will see as you enter Peyriac-Minervois. They carry a serious warning in a colourful and some times amusing way.

Road surfaces are generally good even on minor D roads but they can be very narrow and many French drivers like to drive fast, so be warned! Roadsides in spring and early summer and again in the autumn will be lined with wild flowers. A beautiful sight but remember to keep your eyes on the road! In case of an accident requiring medical assistance, contact the emergency

services: *service d'aide médicale d'urgence* is 15, Police 17 and Fire Pompiers 18.

An increasingly common sight on hill tops or on high ground – some regard them as a blight on the landscape – is a long row of wind turbines *eolliennes*. To the landowners they represent a source of income in a region where more and more vineyards are no longer viable. In some places you can visit the turbines and learn how they are used to generate electricity. One such place is the **Centre d'Essais Éolien** at Portel des Corbières.

As you enter a village there is often a sign indicating how many pedestrian crossings 'passages' there are on the road and how many 'sleeping policemen' '*ralentisseurs*' you will bump over. If there is

something of particular interest in or near the village such as pre-historic dolmens, a pre-Roman iron age hilltop fort or a medieval tower there will usually be a special sign indicating this – like the one pictured left.

In most villages, you can expect to find information boards telling visitors what shops etc are to be found there (see right). You may also find either a map showing the footpaths and marked trails in the immediate vicinity of the village or a colourful map or poster of the wider area (see bottom of page).

An alternative mode of transport is the **autorail touristique du Minervois** which runs in the summer season from Narbonne to Bize Minervois. There is also the **train touristique Trans-Vallées Express** which runs from Rivesaltes in the *département* of Roussillon to Quillan in Aude. This one allows you to get off at a couple of points and make excursions by bus to the Gorges de Galamus and the Castle of

Puilaurans. See www.tpcf.fr

You can also take short flights in small light aircraft either from Carcassonne airport or from the one at Lézignan Corbières.

Seasons of the Year

Carcassonne and the coastal resorts can get very crowded in July and August. If you can come a bit earlier in spring or a bit later in the autumn you will enjoy it even more, and the temperature of the sea is still warm enough for swimming. Christmas too is a good time to visit as lots of extra events are laid on in the lower town. An ice skating rink is rigged up on the *Place Carnot* and there are log cabins selling seasonal fare at a **Marché de Noël**, and there is live music to be enjoyed at it.

Even in the winter months there are special events. Most towns and villages have Christmas markets. The villages of Moussoulens **Map C1**, Talairan **Map D3** and Ville-neuve Minervois **Map C1** each have three **Foires au Truffes** between late December and early February. There is usually a chef at these events describing ways in which to use truffles in your cooking. And there is plenty of other good local produce on sale at them. Puicheric **Map D2** has a pig and wine festival **Fête du cochon et du Minervois** in January.

Many villages arrange communal New Year parties called **Reveillon de Saint Sylvestre**. The local mayors and councils host dinner parties in the New Year for all the senior citizens in their villages. Occasionally, though rarely, there can be a heavy snowfall down on the plain – there's no shortage of it, of course, in the Pyrenees. Not quite what visitors to the Mediterranean may be expecting when they are trying to escape from the cold of northern Europe!

Spring is celebrated with a number of festivals especially in wine villages and at particular *domaines* and *châteaux*. As you drive through villages you will see posters advertising **Printemps du Minervois** and giving the local details. They provide a chance to meet some of the local *vignerons* and sample their products.

C'est le printemps du Minervois

Another spring event is the village **Foire des Fleurs** or flower market where you can stock up on all the flowering plants and bushes you need for the garden or the balcony. The lovely wine village of La Liviniere **Map D1** hosts one in a small park on the edge of town at the beginning of May. Quillan **Map B3** has its in late April. Watch out for signs as you drive into villages about when theirs is. This is sometimes organised as a fund-raiser for the local village school or sports centre. Fontfroide Abbey has a **Fête des Plantes et du Massif** over the weekend 16-17 May.

The harvesting of almost any crop is a good enough reason for a festival, so in May when the first local cherries are appearing, expect to see a **Fête de la Cerise** advertised. The village of Trausse-Minervois **Map D1** has its on May 18th.

These fairs and festivals offer far more than a simple market, though you can of course expect to buy whatever product is being celebrated. They often include lectures on the product, guided walks in the vicinity and the opportunity to share in a public, celebratory meal open to anyone, though booking in advance is usually required.

You will be surprised what can be celebrated! Limoux **Map C2**, for example, has a triennial festival in August in honour of a particular breed of cow, **Fête de la Gasconne**, when the main road through town is lined with temporary cow byres for the weekend and you can enjoy freshly roasted beef sandwiches from street stalls.

Bize-Minervois **Map E1** has its **Fête de l'Olivier** in mid-July. One of the biggest festivals is the **Fête du Cassoulet** at Castelnaudary **Map B1** over the last weekend in August. See www.fete-du-cassoulet.com

Le Village des Producteurs de l'Aude Pays Cathare is an association of forty farmers, winemakers and craftsmen who co-operate in July and August to promote and sell their goods at markets and fairs across the region, from Narbonne Plage and Gruissan on the coast to Limoux, Castelnaudary and Quillan inland.

Village fêtes mark the seasons. Although Church and State are separated in France and many French people are now secular in spirit, Church festivals are still important including that of the local village's saint in whose honour their parish church is dedicated. The Christian festival of All Saints on November 1st is a public holiday and a day when you will see almost all the family graves in the local cemeteries covered in flowers, usually chrysanthemums – see the one pictured on the right. Remembrance Day, November 11th, is a national holiday and there is a short ceremony at the war memorial in most towns and villages – but not always at 11.00, so check the time if you plan to attend.

In the summer many villages lay on street parties open to all. In Villeneuve-Minervois, for example, there is a party once a fortnight on a Tuesday evening open to the whole village and to visitors. It is organised on a different street each time. The format is intense activity during the day by the council workmen as they set up a stage and amplification, and set out rows of chairs. Come the evening there is a public meal followed by entertainment, which may be a group of musicians and singers or a stand-up comedian or some dancing to a band. And a simple bar, of course, on the street. By midnight all is quiet and early next morning the council workmen are back dismantling it all. On Thursdays it is the turn of La Redorte village **Map D2** to do something similar, though their programme includes open air cinema shows as well. And on Fridays it is music and wine night in Caunes Minervois **Map D1**. The village of Pradelles **Map C1** in the Montagne Noire has fireworks and music on three evenings in the summer along with a communal meal. Check in the local tourist office as there may well be something of this kind happening where you are staying – communal celebrations are a feature of village life in this region.

Harvesting the grapes, **Vendange**, which is spread over several weeks is hugely important in village life and when all is safely gathered in, it is time to party. During the harvesting, expect to get stuck on the roads behind small and slow moving tractors (top speed is 25 kph) pulling loads of grapes. Whilst most vineyards have gone over to mechanical picking, a few still do it by hand and all the family get involved. Carcassonne, Lézignan and Limoux all have their **Fête des vins primeurs** in October as do many of the villages in Aude.

Citou **Map D1** celebrates its locally grown sweet onions on the first

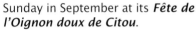

Sunday in September at its **Fête de l'Oignon doux de Citou**.

Mirepoix has its apple festival over a weekend in mid-October – see the picture below. The village of Aigues Vive **Map D2** celebrates three products at the same time at its **Fête de la Pomme, du Vin et du Riz**. Many towns and villages hold a **Foire au Gras** – among them Caunes Minervois and Limoux in November, and Castelnaudary, Belpech and Rieux-Minervois in December. At these you can stock up for Christmas as you will find the pick of locally produced food and drinks on sale at them.

Autumn brings a rich variety of colours in the vineyards – different types of vines turn a different colour: yellow, gold, brown and shades of red, before the leaves fade and fall. Then the cold winter winds blow and nature seems to die. The landscape, however, still looks beautiful, especially on a crystal clear day when you can see the snow-covered Pyrenees shining in the distance.

Relocating to the Region

You have had a wonderful holiday and seen what a very attractive part of France this is. Maybe you spent some time window shopping outside estate agents and picked up some property brochures and now are excitedly contemplating the possibility of moving down here for good.

Take your time before making the decision! It is a huge one and fraught with factors you may not yet have considered sufficiently. It will be worth reading the firsthand accounts of others who have made the move. A good place to start is by subscribing to magazines such as *Living France* or *France* which regularly publish such stories. They also feature excellent articles on the practical aspects of buying and renovating property as well as offering guidance about finance and the French tax and inheritance laws.

Then there are plenty of paperbacks written in the last ten years by expatriates describing their experience. Books such as Rupert Wright's *Notes from the Languedoc* (Ebury Press 2005) and Helena Frith-Powell's *More France please, we're British* sub-titled *15 Lessons on Life in France* (Gibson Square Books 2005). Read them and you will inevitably discover lots about living in the region which at present you don't know, much of it very positive and encouraging but also highlighting some of the very real difficulties which can be encountered, not least if you are hoping to work here. One of the worst obstacles is French bureaucracy. Form-filling and engaging in face-to-face encounters with French officials who do not speak English can be a real headache. If you are not fluent in French, start your language classes at once!

If you are still keen, you may now want to move on to something more technical and detailed such as André de Vries book *Buying a House in France* or the current edition of David Hampshere's *Living & Working in France*, or *The Complete Guide to Living in France* from the publishers of the magazine *Living France*.

If your situation allows you to do it, come and live down here for some weeks out of the normal tourist

season – hiring a *gîte* will be much cheaper than in the summer, and it will give you the opportunity to experience what living in a village or town down here is like as well as giving you plenty of time to explore particular towns and villages where you feel you would be happy and could settle into the local community.

It will also allow you to practise and improve your French and to discover that many of the locals speak a dialect heavily influenced by Occitan! If you are also concerned to establish a network of expatriate friends, there's time to do that. If you take time over the process, you are much more likely to get it right and to make the best decision about where to live.

It might be of help if I tell you how the process of relocating worked out for us. We had visited different parts of France on holiday over the years but found ourselves being drawn back to the Languedoc-Roussillon region again and again, usually in the early autumn when the weather was still good but far fewer visitors were there. At one stage we considered buying a small studio apartment in a new development at the holiday resort of La Bacarès but a year or so later we experienced just how crowded it can get in the high season along the coast and that put us off the idea.

Soon afterwards we decided to explore the possibility of buying an old property inland but sufficiently close to the Mediterranean so that we could easily make day trips

there. We spent one holiday looking at particular towns and villages which appealed to us, some of them in the Roussillon area. For us, one important factor was 'ease of access' meaning was there an airport nearby and preferably one used by low-cost airlines: two such existed at Perpignan and Carcassonne. And both were close to motorways and had mainline railway stations.

We then did a lot of homework via the internet. We spent many an evening accessing the websites of estate agents and looking at properties in our price category. In the end we settled on a long 'short list' of about a dozen properties situated within a 30 mile radius of Carcassonne.

Just after Easter one year, my wife and I flew down to take a closer look at them. Three of them happened to be on the books of the same estate agent in Carcassonne, so we decided to start with that one. We never got any further. We were extremely fortunate in that the member of staff appointed to deal with us spoke excellent English, having lived in the US for some years. She was a model of patience and we spent two and a half days with her driving round and looking at more properties than the three on our list from that agency. They varied quite a lot – the first was a small house in a scenic location high up in the Montagne Noire and needing no renovation at all but it was situated on the edge of a dying village where lots of properties were for sale. Another house which had looked ideal from the pictures on the website turned out to be in a cramped location and right next to a busy road.

One of the properties on our short list was a largish, three-storey village house. We discovered that it had formerly been both the home and the workplace of a *vigneron* and had been empty for many years. *Une petite vigne*, a small parcel of land once covered in vines, went with the house which still had two large wine vats *in situ*. It was located in a lovely village surrounded by vineyards, and clearly a 'living village' with a primary school, several shops, good sports facilities and much to commend it, not least that the residents clearly took pride in the appearance of their village. Among the shops was what one should expect in any good village – a bakery! And a post office.

Unfortunately the only picture of the house on the website had been an exterior one. The reason became obvious when we went inside. It was in need of total renovation which would surely cost far more than the house and land. My wife was appalled by the state of what she saw! But, at the same time, it had distinct attractions and it offered us the possibility of creating the interior in such a way that we would end up with the house we really wanted. Our agent said she remembered seeing some sketches on file back in the office which the previous owner had got an architect to draw, and these she produced for us next day. They looked interesting but first we went looking at other houses before returning to it to have an even closer look. In the absence of any surveyor's report, we then did what most French people do and that is to invite a builder (or architect) to inspect the house with us. One had been recommended to us who specialised in supervising the renovation of old houses. On the basis of her professional advice we

decided to make an offer and sign a *compromis de vente* and pay a deposit. Nowadays, the law allows for a seven day cooling off period in which the buyer can back out but after that the agreement is binding on the purchasers if they don't want to forfeit their deposit.

We chose a *notaire* based in Carcassonne to do the legal work, one that the vendor who lived in Paris was happy to accept. We opened an account with a local bank as soon as we had signed the *compromis de vente* in order to make money transfers easier and to be able to pay all the builders bills with French cheques in euros. The legal work took about three months and we had to transfer the full price plus legal fees to the *notaire* before we all met in her office to initial and sign page after page of the contract. We also had to provide evidence to the notaire that we had insured the house from the date of the transfer of ownership.

Since we bought our house new regulations have come into force which require the seller to provide the purchaser with reports on lead, asbestos, flood zones and in some areas termites. An energy efficiency report and a natural disaster risk report are also now mandatory.

As we would not be living locally during the period of the renovation, we decided to employ a manager for the project who could keep us informed by email of the progress of the work being done by local French artisans. With her help we got fixed-price estimates from three builders, all of whom had recommended totally renewing the roof rather than simply repairing it. We made our choice of builder and fortunately had no reason to regret it over the two years that it took for all the work to be done. We retained a few of the original features in the house but totally changed the layout of the interior.

We chose to do all the work by stages, starting with a new roof and new floors. Each stage entailed a separate fixed price contract with the builder – we paid 20% at the outset and the rest as work was certified completed by the project manager. This helped spread the cost over the whole period and spared us from any cash flow or transfer problems. We flew down on

holiday occasionally but also to see firsthand how the work was coming on. Given that we were living so far away, our employing a local project manager was money well spent. We had a professional to do much of the tiling but some of that work along with the decorations we have done ourselves.

The work of builders and other professionals such as electricians and plumbers is guaranteed for 10 years, and on the couple of occasions when it has been necessary to contact the builder he has come immediately.

Whilst the work was in progress we were spared having to pay the *taxe d'habitation* but we had to pay the annual *taxe foncière* which is based on the size and number of rooms and other facilities in the house. When the work was completed, the house was revalued for taxation purposes which meant a significant increase.

We have had no regrets about the decision we made to buy a house in the region. Our neighbours have been very welcoming and friendly. Developing a network of French and expatriate friends, however, does require effort but it is not too difficult. Villages and towns have large numbers of *associations*, i.e. special interest activity groups, which are glad to welcome new members. If you are a rugby fan, there are some very good teams to follow. And all the usual sporting facilities you would expect to find are here: swimming pools, golf courses, even horse racing!

"No regrets" – I hope that will be your experience too. Two useful websites for people re-locating to the region are www.le-eleven.fr and www.crème-de-languedoc.com *Le Eleven* is also a free monthly English-language magazine. *Languedoc Sun* also publishes a small bi-monthly regional magazine in English which is both free and informative.

8 routes that take in some sites recommended in the Guide

The Michelin regional map is recommended. Road numbers for each route are given but once you leave the D6113, the main road out of Carcassonne, their numbers change so often you may find it easier to simply look for the name of the next village on your route on the signposts. There are lots of places to visit on each route, so you may well prefer to miss out some and spend longer at just a few of them.

Tour 1: Lagrasse, the Corbières hills, the castles at Queribus, Peyrepertuse and Puilaurens, the Gorges de Galamus & the Défilé de la Pierre-Lys.

You will need to start early if you are going to visit all the sites suggested. It is a long drive (about 130 miles) but with lots of interesting places to see, starting with one of the most beautiful villages in France followed by some spectacular castles and wonderful scenery.

Leave Carcassonne on the D6113 signposted to Narbonne. Just before Trèbes, turn right on to the D3 signposted to **Lagrasse** (see pages 10 + 41). From Lagrasse take the D212 south, turn left on to the D23 and then right on to the D613 signposted to **Villerouge-Termenès** (see page 9). Carry on to Félines-Termenès, past the village turn left on to the D39, then D139 signposted to Davejean, D410 to Maisons, D123 to Padern, D14 to Cucugnan, and the D123 to the **Château de Queribus** (see page 8). Go back down the hill and back down the D123, turn left on to the D14 to Duilhac-sous-Peyrepertuse. Park below the castle and climb up to the **Château de Peyrepertusé** (see page 8).

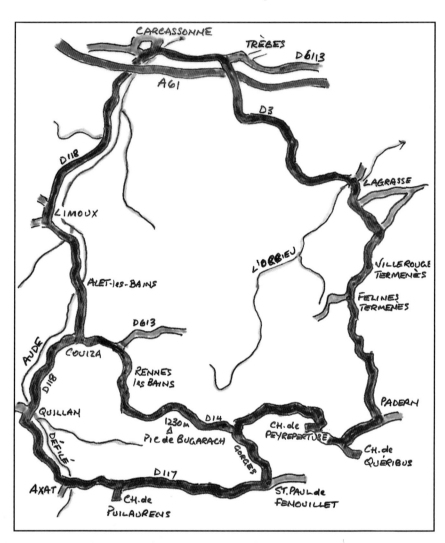

Back to the D14 and carry on to Cubières-sur-Cinoble, turn left on to the D10 for the **Gorges de Galamus** (see page 27) and the Ermitage St-Antoine de Galamus, then the D7 to St-Paul-de-Fenouillet, where you turn right on to the D117. At Lapradelle turn left on to the D22 for the **Château de Puilaurens**, park and climb up to the castle (see page 8). Back to the D117 and turn left for Axat, join the D118 signposted to Quillan, drive through the narrow **Défilé de la Pierre-Lys**. After Quillan follow the signs for Limoux via Espéraza, Couiza and Alet-les-Bains. Stay on the D118 through the large town of Limoux and follow the signs for Carcassonne.

An alternative and shorter route (marked in dark blue on the map) for the last part of the journey would be to carry on along the D14 after Cubières-sur-Cinoble to Bugarach and Rennes-les-Bains (stop for a swim in the open air thermal pool), turning left at the junction with the D613 which brings you to Couiza and the D118 for Limoux and Carcassonne. This route takes you through some beautiful upland scenery around Bugarach though at times the road is very winding and you cannot afford to let the scenery affect your concentration on the road!

Tour 2: The Lastours castles, the paper mill at Brousses-et-Villaret, the waterfall at Cubserviès, the leisure area at Pradelles, the Lama farm and the Gouffre de Cabrespine.

This tour is about 65 miles long. Take the D118 from Carcassonne north signposted Mazamet, turn left on to the D103 to **Brousses-et-Villaret** (see page 23). Return to the D118, turn right heading back in the direction of Carcassonne until the junction with the D111 signposted to Villardonnel and Salsigne and **Lastours** (see page 9). Park in the free car park soon after entering the village and walk to the Visitors Centre (housed in a former mill) at the foot of the steep climb up to the four castles. You need to be fairly fit for this! See the exhibition of photos in the Centre. Lunch at the restaurant outside or at the auberge by the gourmet restaurant *Le Puits du Trésor*. You can get some good photos looking up the hill but for a panoramic picture of all four drive up to the view point at Belvédère de Montfermier above the village.

After lunch head north on D101 along the gorge of the River Orbiel to Roquefère. Turn left up a steep and narrow winding road (not one for the faint hearted!) to the *Cascade de Cubserviès*. There is limited parking by the viewpoint just above the waterfall which is one of the highest in Europe. Continue 1½ kilometres to the 12th century **Chapel of St Sernin**, on to the D1009 and D9 to **Pradelles Cabardès** for the leisure area there (see pages 16–17) – a man-made lake for swimming, walking, picnicking, etc – then either detour up the D87 to the highest point, the **Pic de Nore** at 1211m for amazing views as far as the Pyrenees or take the D89 signposted Castans and the D9 to the **Lama farm** (see page 18).

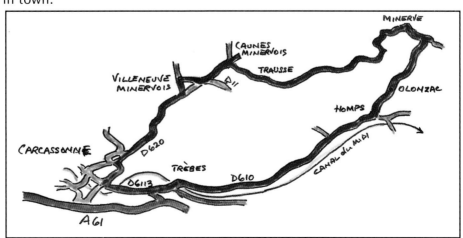

Return to the D112 and follow the gorge of the River Clamoux to the village of Cabrespine and a kilometre past it to the giant cavern *Gouffre de Cabrespine* (see page 26) – where the last guided tour of the day is at 17.00, then on to Villeneuve-Minervois . The D112 out of the village joins up with D620 back to Carcassonne 16 kms away. The last part runs alongside the *Canal du Midi* and passes one of the out-of-town shopping centres at *Pont Rouge*. The unmanned petrol station (credit cards only) here usually has the cheapest petrol in town.

Tour 3: The mill at Villeneuve Minervois, the abbey & marble quarry at Caunes Minervois, the village of Minerve, the Canal du Midi and Chai at Homps, and Lake Jouarres.

This tour is about 70 miles. Take the road out of

Carcassonne signposted for Mazamet, at a major roundabout take the D620 signposted Villalier, Villegly and Caunes Minervois. Turn off left on to the D112 for **Villeneuve-Minervois** and follow the signs for the **Moulin** (see page 22). On leaving, drive through the village centre and follow the sign for **Caunes Minervois**, the D111, back to the D620, turn left for Caunes (see pages 40-41). Follow the sign for *centre ville* and the car park in front of the mairie. It is a short walk to the Abbey (see page 10) and then up the hill to the potter's studio. Return to the car park and go back to the main road through the town, the D620, and on the outskirts of town turn left along a track for the car park near the marble quarries, which are just a short walk away. Return to the town centre to find the D115 signposted for Trausse and on to the junction with the D52, turn left and follow the signs for Siran, Cesseras, Azillanet and **Minerve** (see page 41). Parking is outside the village close to the bridge giving access to it. From Minerve continue on the D115 to La Caunette and on to the junction with the D907 signposted to Aigues-Vives, turn right down a short minor road to Aigne and turn right on the D910 signposted to Beaufort, Olonzac and **Homps**. The roads in the village centre of Homps can be confusing as well as narrow but follow the signs for the Canal and you will soon arrive outside the old warehouse which is now the Chai, the centre for Minervois wines (see page 14). You can take a ride on a canal boat from here or hire a cycle to ride along the Canal. Or if you fancy a swim, **Jouarres Lake** (see page 16) is just a mile away with a sandy beach. Return to Carcassonne via the D610 to Puichéric and Trèbes where you meet the D6113.

Tour 4: The wine-making museum at Lézignan-Corbières, Fontfroide Abbey, the honey centre at Montseret and the beach at Port-la-Nouvelle.

Take the D6113 out of Carcassonne signposted Narbonne and turn off at **Lézignan-Corbières** for the town centre. There is a traditional market here on Wednesdays. The museum (see page 23) is close to the railway station (*Gare SNCF*). Take the D24 out of town signposted to Cruscades and Bizanet, the road becomes the D224, at

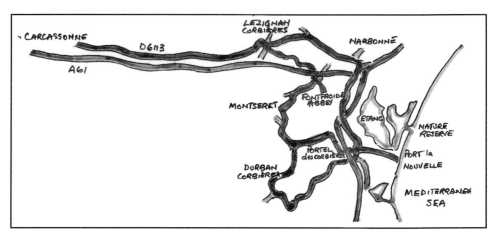

Bizanet follow the signs for **Abbey de Frontfroide**; the road is a minor one which crosses the D613 shortly before the Abbey (see page 11).

On leaving, go back to the D613, turn left on to it and go as far as the junction with the D423 signposted to St André-de-Roquelongue, turn left on to this road which leads to **Montseret** where you will see signs for the **Miellerie des Clauses** (see page 32). Take the D123 to Donos, turn left on to the D611 to Montplaisir, carry on to the junction with the D611A, turn left on to it and head for **Portel-des-Corbières** and the **Terra Vinea** (see page 15) subterranean wine caves which are well signposted. Take the D3 to Sigean which for a short stretch merges with the D6139 signposted **Port-la-Nouvelle** (see pages 20-21). If you prefer a walk in a nature reserve rather than spending time on the beach, the track to the **Ile de Ste Lucie** (see page 24) is on the left as you are entering the port, you need to take the road bridge over the canal to get to it. If you want the beach, head straight on with the canal on your left. Return via the D6139 to the D6009 signposted Narbonne and pick up the D6113 back to Carcassonne.

An alternative to the winery and the beach is to do a circuit in the Corbières (marked in dark blue on the map) enjoying the scenery and seeing some of the wine villages: take the D611 down to Durban-Corbières, on to Villeneuve-les-Corbières, then on to the D205 to Embres-et-Castelmaure, St Jean-de-Barrou, Fraissé-des-Corbières and follow the signs for Sigean; you will meet the D6009 just before Sigean, head for Narbonne where you will see signs for the D6113 and Carcassonne. Each route is about 130 miles.

Tour 5: St Hilaire Abbey, Limoux & the Aude valley, Puivert Castle & Lake Montbel

This route is about 90 miles. Follow the signs out of Carcassone for Limoux which will bring you on to the D118. After Rouffic-d'Aude turn left on to the D110 signposted Pomas and St-Hilaire (see page 10) where parking is a short walk away from the abbey. Take the D104 signposted for Limoux (see page 40). There is parking off the main road, the D118, across from the tourist office and the Petiet Art

Museum, and it's just a short walk down in to the town centre. Afterwards, head south on the D118 along the valley of the River Aude where you can hire a kayak or go water rafting (see page 16) to Alet, then on to Couiza where you can make a detour on the D52 up the mountain to Rennes-le-Chateau made famous by the novel and film *The da Vinci Code*. Then comes **Espéraza** with its dinosaur museum and hat factory museum (see page 22). The dinosaur trail is nearby at Campagne-sur-Aude. At Quillan, turn right on to the D117 signposted to Nébias and **Puivert** for the castle with its 35 m high keep and Quercorb Museum (see page 23). There is a small lake with a beach close to the village centre, if you fancy a swim. Take the D120 signposted to Rivel and on to the junction with the D620, turn left for Ste-Colombe-sur-l'Hers, and turn left on to a minor road signposted for **Montbels** which will bring you to the lake (see page 16). Take the D18 signposted to **Chalabre** (see page 19), which after the town becomes the D620 and leads to Limoux town centre where, if you didn't do it earlier, you should stop and taste some the town's famous sparkling wine (see page 15). The D118 takes you back to Carcassonne.

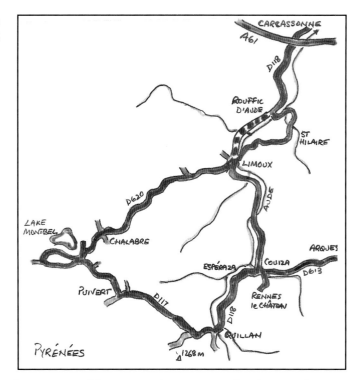

An alternative route after Couiza is to take the D613 (marked in dark blue on the map) and head out to **Arques** (see page 34) to see the castle there, and take a walk in the forests nearby. You could also combine this with the detour to Rennes-le-Château mentioned above. Return back along the D613 to Couiza, turn right on to the D118 and head back to Limoux and Carcassonne.

Tour 6: Narbonne, the Clape massif, Narbonne Plage and Amphoralis at Sallèles d'Aude.

This route is about 105 miles. Take the D6113 from Carcassonne to **Narbonne**. Park in the town centre near the open air market (see page 41) for easy access to the

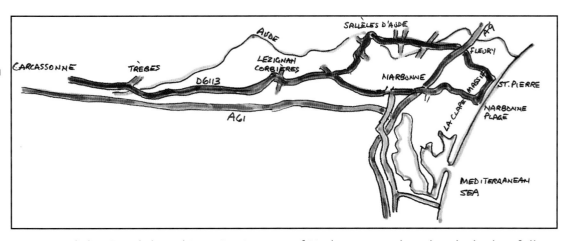

cathedral and museums and the Canal de Robine. Getting out of Narbonne can be a headache but follow the signs for *autres directions* until you see a sign for **Narbonne Plage** which should lead you on to the D168 over the **La Clape massif** and past the **Château de l'Hospitalet** (see page 34) before you drop down to the coast. Turn left heading in the direction of St Pierre and turn off right to park by the beach (see page 21). In St Pierre take the D1118 inland and you will come to a tree-shaded parking area on the right hand side of the road not far from the **Gouffre de l'Œil-Doux** (see page 27). Continue on the D1118 to Fleury and Salles-d'Aude where you turn left on to the D31 for Coursan where you join and cross the D009 to pick up the D1118 for Cuxac-d'Aude and on to **Salleles-d'Aude** for the Roman pottery museum and the Patchwork Centre by the Canal (see page 22). Back to the D1118 to St-Marcel-sur-Aude, then left on to the D607 to Marcorignan and a minor road which links to the D6113 signposted to Lézignan-Corbières, and on to Carcassonne.

Tour 7: African Safari Park and the beaches at Port-La-Nouvelle/Leucate Plage

This tour is about 140 miles but almost entirely along fast, major roads. Take the D6113 in the direction of Narbonne and on the outskirts join the D6009 signposted for Perpignan or take the motorways A61 and A9 down to junction 39. After the turning for Peyriac-sur-Mer on the D6009 comes the signpost for the **Réserve Africaine** (see page 19), turn left on to the approach road to it. If you haven't already visited Terra Vinea at Portel-les-Corbières, you can do that after the Safari Park – the D611A leads to it. Take the road back to the D6009 and head south for the beaches – either to **Port-la-Nouvelle** (see pages 20-21) if you haven't already been there or go a bit further south to the resorts at **Leucate Plage** and **Port Leucate** (see page 20) via the D627.

The closest of the resorts on this stretch of the coastline is **La Franqui Plage** north of **Cap Leucate**. You get to it from the D6009 via the D627 and the D427. Return to Carcassonne either via the motorway which you can access at junction 40 or by the D6009 and the D6113.

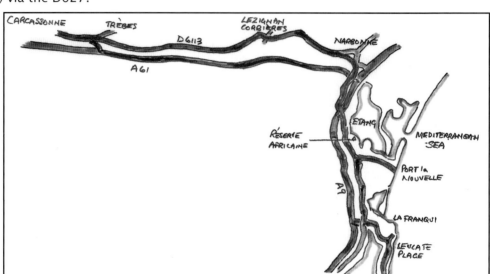

Tour 8:
Montolieu, Saissac Castle, St Papoul Abbey, Castelnaudary, Mirepoix and Montréal.

This tour is about 75 miles long. Leave Carcassonne heading west on the D6113, after Pezens fork right on to the D629 to the book town of **Montolieu** (see page 41) and on to the castle at **Saissac**. Not far away is the deer farm at Picarel le Haut (see page 18). From Saissac take the D103 signposted to **St Papoul** (see page 10). You can park in the square right outside the Abbey. Continue on the D103 into the centre of **Castelnaudary** (see page 40). If you haven't yet feasted on *cassoulet*, this is the place to do so. Take the D6 out of the town south to the beautiful, medieval town of **Mirepoix** (see page 40) where there are some good shops in the square by the cathedral.

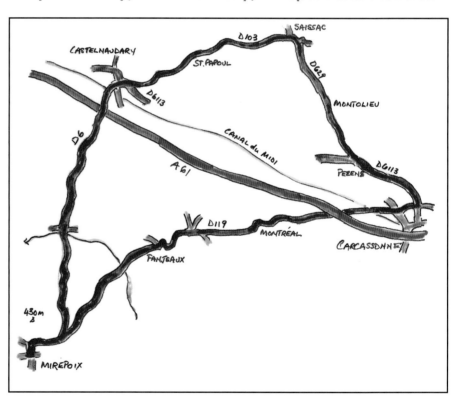

Return to Carcassonne via Fanjeaux where St Dominic founded his first religious community and via Montréal. **Montréal** was where Cathar and Catholic theologians met in 1207 to argue the merits of their faiths – Dominic took part on the Catholic side. The town's Collegiate Church of St Vincent with its vast Gothic nave and beautiful 18th century organ is worth a visit. The church was founded by Pope Jean XXII in 1317.

Practical Information

When to go

If the weather is a major consideration for you in determining when to visit, here is an overview of average temperatures and rainfall through the year. May and September are lovely months in which to come not least because there are fewer visitors and there is much less traffic on the main roads to and along the coast.

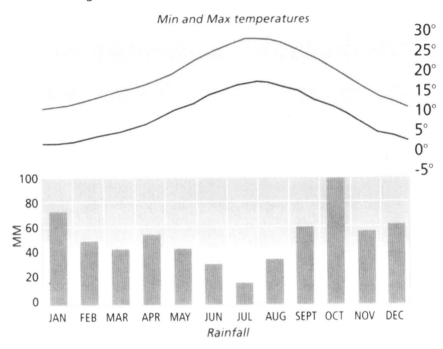

Getting there

By Air:

There are direct flights to Carcassonne with Ryanair from Charleroi, Cork, Dublin, Shannon, Edinburgh, East Midlands Airport near Nottingham, Liverpool and London Stansted Airport. See www.ryanair.com for booking.

The airport website www.carcassonne. aeroport.fr/ (French) also gives an overview of schedules in addition to other useful information. The airport is compact and easy to find your way around. You will find an information point, an ATM, car hire desks, a restaurant and a small shop which stocks books written by ex-pats. There is a short stay car park just across the road from the main entrance which is free for the first 30 minutes.

Other Airports:

Other airports within reasonable distance of Carcassonne are Perpignan, Béziers. Toulouse and Montpellier. There are direct flights from the UK with Ryanair (London Stansted – Perpignan and to Béziers), BMI Baby (Manchester – Perpignan) and Flybe (Southampton & Birmingham – Perpignan). Montpellier airport is served by Ryanair from London Stansted and by British Airways from Gatwick. See www.perpignan.cci.fr and www.montpellier.aeroport.fr Toulouse is about 90km from Carcassonne and is a major international airport with several airlines flying to it from the UK. See the airport website www.toulouse.aeroport.fr

By Train:

Carcassonne station is located in the centre of the lower town. For all train information see the website for the French railway SNCF at www.sncf.fr

There are direct day and night trains from Paris (Austerlitz) to Carcassonne. It is possible to take your car by motorail from Calais to Toulouse or Narbonne. This isn't cheap, but depending on how long you are staying in the area and how many of you are traveling, it might make sense financially and you will certainly arrive more rested. See: www.raileurope.co.uk International rail tickets can also be purchased at this website. Tickets for the trains from London St Pancras to Paris Gard du Nord via the Channel Tunnel can be booked from www.eurostar.com

By Car:

It is a very long drive from any of the Channel ports to Carcassonne – the routes from Calais, Boulogne or Dunkirk using the motorways south all take about 10 hours driving (excluding stops for rest and refreshment). From St Malo it is shorter but the Channel crossing takes much longer and is more expensive. For help with routes, see www.theaa.com, www.rac.co.uk, www.mappy.com and www.viamichelin.com It is best to break the journey half way – there are plenty of cheap hotels situated close to motorway junctions. I prefer to use the Channel tunnel train from Folkestone to Calais; it is fast and with convenient access to motorways on both sides of the Channel. See www.eurotunnel.com for details of times and prices. I often use the French motorail service from Calais to Toulouse or the other way as a rest from driving. If you prefer to cross by ferry, the Norfolk Line www.norfolkline.com which runs from Dover to Dunkirk is among the cheapest.

Getting around

To / from the Airport:

A shuttle bus (*navette*) runs to / from the centre of Carcassonne stopping at the railway station *Gare SNCF* (**Town map B1**), Place Davilla (**map A2**), Square Gambetta (**map C2**) – the fare is €5. The timetable for the shuttle bus is available online at www.carcassonne.org under *Practical Information / Transport*, and on the airport website or you can get the timetable from the tourist office. Taxis are also available at the airport and the fare to town is around 10 euros. Phone radio taxi Service 04 68 25 28 18.

Getting around Carcassonne:

Agglo provides the municipal bus service between 07.00 and 19.30. For details ring *Halte Centrale Agglo bus* : 04.68.47.82.22. A network map and timetables can be viewed online at www.carcassonne.org Alternatively the tourist office will give you information on how to get where you want to go. A single ticket costs €1.10 cents and is valid for 1 hour, a day ticket costs 2.50 and allows an unlimited number of journeys, a carnet of 10 single tickets costs 7.80. From mid-June to mid-September, a shuttle bus runs between the *Cité* and the lower town (*Les Halles*) every 15 minutes. A return ticket for this service costs €1,50, children under 7 travel free. In the past, from the beginning of May to mid-October, there has been free transport round the lower city by small electric vehicles called *toucs* but these may not be in service in 2009. A taxi rank is to be found near the railway station, but remember that most taxis will only take three passengers – tel: 04 68 71 50 50.

Getting around the region:
A *navette* from the airport to the upper valley of the Aude calls at Limoux, Alet-les-Bains, Couiza, Espéraza and Quillan - for booking see www.aerobus-hautevallee.com or phone 04 68 20 15 54. A couple of regional bus services will get you to / from villages and towns around Carcassonne. These include Cars Teissier and TransAude. Car Teissier has a website: www.teissier.fr with information on their regular bus schedule and guided bus tours. More information on regional travel is available from the tourist office or the bus companies. Between June and October the tourist office also runs a number of guided bus tours to some popular sites in the region. These are not cheap, however, 30 – 40 euros per adult, children under 15 half price, children under 6 free, more information on www.carcassonne.org or from the tourist office. Information about regional rail services is available at www.ter-sncf.com or from the railway station in Carcassonne (**Town map B1**) – tel:04 68 71 79 14. There are a dozen trains a day to Narbonne and even more in the opposite direction to Toulouse, and five a day up the Aude Valley to Limoux, two of which go further to Quillan.

Car Hire:
It is possible to get around the city and further afield using public transport. However, you might like to list which sites you want to visit and do some research to find out if these destinations can be conveniently reached by public transport. If you wish to do a lot of touring in the region hiring a car is a convenient option. Car hire firms have offices at Carcassonne Airport and in the city centre. If you are arriving on a Ryanair flight, it is worth looking at the cost of hiring a car through their partner Hertz, see www.ryanair.com Pre-booking a car is not a bad idea whichever firm you use as the queues at the car hire desks at the airport can sometimes be bothersome. Otherwise, you can always jump on the *navette* and hire a car in the city centre. Ada and Hertz have offices conveniently located on *Boulevard Omer Saurraut* opposite the railway station. A number of other companies have offices dotted around the city centre. Remember that most shops and offices close for lunch between 12 – 14.00.

Canal Cruiser Hire:
Cruising along the *Canal du Midi* is a wonderfully relaxing way to see part of the region. Cruisers can be hired from a number of locations – see www.croisieres-du-midi.com or www.audetourisme.com for details.

Cycle Hire:
Cycling is a very popular sport in France, more so than probably anywhere else in Europe, so you will find cycling routes publicised by the local tourist offices in many parts of *Aude*, and you can hire cycles in many of the towns – Carcassonne, Narbonne, Trèbes, Homps and Bram among them. Philippe Calas set up a web site in 1999 for people wanting to cycle the length of the *Canal du Midi* – see www.canalmidi.com – and two years later wrote a guide book for cyclists *Le Canal du Midi à Vélo*. See also www.vtt-pyreness.com and www.cycleaude.com for cycling holidays in the upper valley of the River Aude.

Accommodation
Hotels which are part of the cheapest chains such as *Formule* 1 and *Etap* are usually located on the outskirts of town – expect to pay about 30-35€ for a room, breakfast is extra. One chain which has hotels of various levels of comfort and cost is www.accorhotels.com. *Logis de France* are mid-range-priced and usually family-run hotels, see www.logisdefrance.com for bookings and www.logisdefrance-aude.com for details of their local hotels. There is a good overview of accommodation possibilities with contact details at www.carcassonne.org It is possible to find a room in the *Cité* itself even if you are on a limited budget.

To book a *gîte*, see www.gites-de-france-aude.com where you can get details of properties in the *département* of Aude and also of people registered to provide Bed + Breakfast *Chambres d'Hôtes*. A room in B + B houses is likely to cost between 45€ and 65€ a night, though some are cheaper and a few are much more expensive. Some owners also offer an evening meal *Tables d'Hôtes* at an extra charge but not all do this. The agency has a brochure giving details of all those registered with them and their grading and price. The grades are marked with one to four arrowheads and you will find a plaque outside each registered property showing its grade.

There are also a number of advertising agencies which provide details of properties for hire, such as www.bvdirect.co.uk, www.cheznous.com, and www.ownersinfrance.com but they do not take responsibility for the quality of the properties and you have to rely on the owner's description being accurate. After that cautionary note I must add that on the one occasion when I booked some *gîtes* in the Corbières so that all three generations of our family could be together, I found the properties and the pool to be even better than the website had described them!

During the winter months if you are thinking of a weekend break in Carcassonne, you can benefit from the **2 nuits d'hôtel pour le prix d'1** offer which is available in a number of French cities. Eight 2 and 3 star hotels in Carcassonne belong to the scheme. See www.villepassion.fr or www.carcassonne-tourisme.com for more information.

The Aude Tourist Board publishes a 20 page booklet **Tourisme & Handicap** listing hotels, restaurants and other sites which have wheelchair access and which make provision for those with other disabilities.

Public holidays/*Jours feriés*

January 1	*Jour de l'An*/New Year's Day
May 1	*Fête de Travail*/Labour Day
May 8	*Fête de la Victoire 1945*/Victory Day
July 14	*Fête Nationale*/Bastille Day
August 15	*Assomption*/Assumption of the Blessed Virgin Mary
November 1	*Fête de Toussaint*/All Saints
November 11	*Jour de l'Armistice*/ Remembrance Day
December 25	*Noël*/Christmas Day

and other major Christian festivals which have variable dates: *Pâcques*/Easter (and Easter Monday), Ascension and *Pentecôte*/ Whitsunday. Shops do not open on these days.

Church Services

Local parish churches are Roman Catholic and services are, of course, in French. Both Carcassonne and Narbonne have cathedrals. Mass is usually celebrated at 11.00 on Sundays but also at other times and often on Saturday evenings. There is an English-language Anglican congregation in Limoux with Sunday services at 10.30 – see www.escotc.com There is also an English language Protestant service every Sunday morning in Homps at 10.30. It is held in the restaurant *Les Tonneliers* by the canal. See www.christiansinaude.org

Local Tourist Information Offices

Unfortunately, not all tourist offices have websites where you can access local information but all of them do stock a wide range of informative brochures. In the country they are still often called *syndicat d'Initiative*; in towns they are usually called *office de tourisme*. See the next Unit for website details. Do visit the ones in villages too – you could end up taking part in some very enjoyable local event.

If you are planning to visit more than four of the Cathar Country sites it is worth buying an *Intersite* card (3 euros) which gives you a 1 euro reduction at each of the 19 sites covered by the card. It is even better value for children as admission to all the sites is free for children with a card. Reductions in admission charges at other tourist sites are usually only given to children and students.

Emergencies

Make sure you have the EU health cover card with you and show it if you have to visit a GP, hospital, clinic or dentist – you can normally obtain about 70% reimbursement on presentation of your receipted bills at the local CPAM office – the refund is sent to you later at your home address. If you are driving to the hospital look out for the road signs: usually a large letter H in red with a smaller red cross and an arrow indicating which way to turn. The Saturday local papers give details of which chemists are open over the weekend – in *Midi Libre* look for *EN CAS D'URGENCE* where you will find all the essential phone numbers for the emergency services, hospitals, chemists, etc.

Three numbers worth noting are:
Emergency medical aid *SAMU service d'aide médicale d'urgence* **is 15,**
Police 17 and Fire *Pompiers* **18**

5 good books to wet your appetite

A novel – *Labyrinth* Kate Mosse Orion 2006
A history of the Cathars – *The perfect Heresy* Stephen O'Shea Profile Books 2000
About life in the region – *Notes from the Languedoc* Rupert Wright Ebury Press 2005
Two beautifully illustrated French guide books are *Aude, Pays Cathare* Guides Gallimard 2006 and *Evasion Pays Cathare* Hachette 2008

Some language basics

Do not expect to find shopkeepers or the staff at the sites you visit fluent in English. They are much more likely to expect you to have some knowledge of French and when you do try to speak it – however badly - you will find that they will then all the more willingly try out their limited English. Why not brush up your French or do a basic course in the months before you travel? Your local FE centre may run conversational classes in French. Or if you prefer to study

at your own pace, there are several courses available from bookshops – BBC Active French has a CD course for absolute beginners and a second one for those wanting to improve their language skills – each one costs £14.99. There is additional help to be gained from the BBC's website www.bbc.co.uk/languages/french . Rosetta Stone's award-winning language learning software is another option; see their website www.RosettaStone.co.uk You can find many more if you do a search on the internet. At the very least I recommend that you buy a simple phrase book and learn how to greet people, how to ask for directions or order a meal in a restaurant, etc.

Failing all else, you have the absolute bare minimum on page 60. And as you explore the region, you will quickly begin to recognise and understand words and phrases that you see on signs and posters and shops. You can probably guess what this sign on the left is saying to motorists.

Useful Websites
Most – but not all – of these sites have an English language version

Tourism

www.audetourisme.com

www.aude-en-pyrenees.fr

www.carcassonne.org

www.tourisme-corbieres-minervois.com

www.hautescorbieres.com

www.payscathare.org

Accommodation

www.bienvenue-a-la-ferme.com

www.gites-de-france-aude.com

www.logis-de-france-aude.com

Transport

www.aerobus-hautevallee.com

www.carcassonne.aeroport.fr

www.flybe.com

www.flybmi.com

www.ryanair.com

www.raileurope.co.uk

www.eurostar.com

www.eurotunnel.com

www.sncf.fr

www.ter-sncf.com

www.tpcf.fr

www.norfolkline.com

www.rac.co.uk

www.theaa.com

www.viamichelin.com

www.croisieres-du-midi.com

Particular tourist sites

www.castelnautique.com

www.abbaye-de-villelongue.com

www.carcassonne.culture.fr (for a virtual tour of the *Cité*)

www.chateau-arques.fr

www.chateau-chalabre.com

www.chateau-peyrepertuse.com

www.chateau-de-puivert.com

www.chemindesartistes.com

www.citedesoiseaux.com

www.fontfroide.com

www.labouichere.com

www.lagrasse.com

www.lamabalade.fr

http://leparcaustralien.free.fr

www.loulibo.com

www,midicanal.fr

www.miellerie-des-clauses.com

www.montolieu.net

www.parc-naturel-narbonnaise.fr

www.picarel-cerf.com

www.quercorb.com

www.queribus.fr

www.rennes-le-chateau.fr

www.reserveafricainesigean.fr

http://saintpapoul.free.fr

Museums

www.dinosauria.org

www.hautpoul.org (for the Toy Museum)

www.moulinapapier.com

www.moulin-benazeth.fr

www.museecanaldumidi.fr

www.musee-chevalerie.com

www.patchwork-cep.com

Music

www.festivaldecarcassonne.com

www.carcassonne-festivaldelabastide.com

www.estivales.org (for organ concerts in the *Cité*)

www.festival-fontcalvy.com

www.fugueenauderomane.fr

www.jazz-roquefere.com

www.fontfroide.com

Outdoor Activities

www.aude-en-pyrenees.fr

www.audescapades.com

www.cycleaude.com

www.eau-rizon.org

www.espaceliberte.com

www.gruissan-windsurf.com

www.mellowvelos,com

www.mondial-du-vent.com

www.02aventure.spaces.live.com

www.sudwindsports.com

www.vtt-pyrenees.com

Wine

www.aoc-cabardes.com

www.aoc-corbieres.com

www.chateaudeschanoines.com

www.chateaudelastours.com

www.chateaustjacques.com

www.laclape.com

www.cru-fitou.com

www.languedoc-wines.com

www.laurancabaret.com

www.lechai-portminervois.com

www.leminervois.com

www.limoux-aoc.com

www.terra-vinea.com

www.vins-malepere.com

The Coast

www.gruissan-mediterranee.com

www.leucate.net

www.narbonne-plage.com

www.portlanouvelle.com

Some Tourist Offices

http://info.aletlesbains.free.fr

www.carcassonne-tourisme.com

www.castelnaudary-tourisme.com

www.caunesminervois.com

www.corbieres-sauvages.com

www.hautminervois.fr

www.lezignan-corbieres.fr/tourisme

www.limoux.fr

www.montreal-aude.fr

www.narbonne.latitude-gallimard.com

www.paysdecouiza.fr

www.portel-des-corbieres.org

www.renneslesbains.org

www.salleles-daude.com

www.villeneuve-minervois.com

www.ville-quillan.fr

Better a little French than none at all

And assuming you still remember the correct pronunciation from your schooldays!

bonjour	hello, good day
bonsoir	good evening
s'il vous plaît (svp)	please
merci	thank you
d'accord	OK
au revoir	goodbye
oui	yes
non	no

At a cafe/restaurant

je voudrais ...	I would like ...
une table pour deux personnes svp	
	a table for two, please
une bière svp	a beer please
pression/en bouteille	draught/bottle (beer)
un grand café crème	coffee with milk
un thé au lait svp	tea with milk please
une glace au chocolat	a chocolate ice
le menu fixe svp	the set menu, please
je prends le menu à vingt euros	
	I'll take the 20 euro menu
un pichet du vin rouge	a jug of the house red
qu'est-ce que c'est?	what's this?
Je suis végétarien	I am a vegetarian
qu'est ce que vous recommendez?	
	what do you recommend?
c'est tout	that's all
c'est combien?	how much is it?
l'addition, svp	the bill, please
c'est bon	that's fine
il y a une erreur	there's a mistake

Asking for directions

où est ....?	where is ....?
à gauche	on the left
à droite	on the right
tout droit	straight ahead
c'est loin?	Is it far?
la banque	the bank
la cathédrale	the cathedral
le château	the castle
le centre-ville	the town centre
la gare	the station
l'hôpital	the hospital
le marché	the market
le musée	the museum
la piscine	the swimming pool
la plage	the beach
la poste	the post office
Il y a une pharmacie près d'ici?	
	Is there a chemist near here?
où sont les toilettes?	where are the toilets?

Some road signs

autoroute	motorway
péage	toll
sortie	exit
cédéz le passage	give way
ralentissez	slow down

fermé	closed
ouvert	open
occupé	engaged
en panne	out of order
eau potable	drinking water
réservé aux riverains	residents' parking only
la navette	shuttle service

Other useful words and phrases

Avez-vous ?	do you have any..?
je peux goûter?	may I taste some?
je voudrais louer...	I'd like to hire a...
pouvez vous m'aider?	can you help me?
à quelle heure est ...?	at what time is ...?
au secours!	help!
aujourd'hui	today
demain	tomorrow
hier	yesterday
nous sommes en vacances	we are on holiday
nous sommes d'Angleterre/d'Irlande	
	we are from England/Ireland
désolé, je ne parle pas français	
	I'm sorry, I don't speak French
je ne comprends pas	I don't understand
parlez lentement svp	please speak slowly
parlez vous anglais?	do you speak English?

Numbers

1	un	11	onze	21	vingt-et-un
2	deux	12	douze	30	trente
3	trois	13	treize	40	quarente
4	quatre	14	quatorze	50	cinquante
5	cinq	15	quinze	60	soixante
6	six	16	seize	70	soixante-dix
7	sept	17	dix-sept	80	quatre-vingts
8	huit	18	dix-huit	90	quatre-vingt-dix
9	neuf	19	dix-neuf	100	cent
10	dix	20	vingt	200	deux cents

Days of the Week

Sunday	dimanche
Monday	lundi
Tuesday	mardi
Wednesday	mercredi
Thursday	jeudi
Friday	vendredi
Saturday	samedi

Some other signs

stationnement interdit	no parking
stationnement payant	pay to park
boue après orage	muddy road after a storm
verglas fréquent	often (black) ice
route barrée	road closed

Roadside near Limoux in the summer

Château et remparts de Carcassonne

1 Entrée du château
2 Basilique Saint-Nazaire et Saint-Celse
3 Porte Narbonnaise
4 Porte d'Aude
5 Porte Saint-Nazaire
6 Théâtre Jean Deschamps
7 Puits

Vous êtes ici
You are here / Están aquí

Office de Tourisme
Tourist Office

Toilettes
Toilets

Téléphone
Public phone

La cour d'honneur du château est accessible
The main courtyard is accessible

Remparts accessibles à partir du château
Ramparts accessible via the castle

Votre parcours

La cité de Carcassonne du 12ᵉ siècle est dominé par le château des seigneurs Trencavel. Au siècle suivant, elle est annexée au domaine royal, et les représentants du roi de France en renforcent les défenses.

A l'intérieur du château un film sur grand écran évoque l'histoire de la cité de l'époque romaine jusqu'aux restaurations du 19ᵉ siècle. Le parcours sur le chemin de ronde permet de découvrir les systèmes de défense médiévaux et d'admirer le paysage. Les salles accueillent une collection de sculptures provenant de Carcassonne et de ses environs, ainsi que les peintures murales du donjon des Trencavel. Des visites accompagnées sur les remparts sont régulièrement proposées.

Visit the Castle

The 12ᵗʰ-century walled city of Carcassonne is dominated by the feudal castle of the Trencavel family. In the following century it was annexed as royal property and the representatives of the King of France strengthened its defences. Inside the castle a film about the history of the walled city from the Roman period to the 19ᵗʰ century is shown on a wide screen. The mediaeval defences can be seen from the rampart walk which also affords a magnificent view of the countryside. A collection of sculptures from Carcassonne and its environs is exhibited in the building, together with painted murals in the Trencavel family keep. Guided tours of the ramparts are available.

Recorrido del castillo

La Cité de Carcasona del siglo XII está dominada por el castillo de los señores Trencavel. En el siglo siguiente, fue anexionada a las posesiones reales y, los representantes del rey de Francia refuerzan las defensas.

Dentro del castillo, una película en una gran pantalla evoca la historia de la ciudad de la época romana hasta las restauraciones del siglo XIX. El recorrido por el camino de ronda permite descubrir los sistemas de defensa medievales y admirar el paisaje. Las salas acogen una colección de esculturas procedentes de Carcasona y de sus alrededores, así como las pinturas murales del torreón de los Trencavel. Puede accederse a las murallas mediante visita acompañada.

9 780950 832531

£6.00 in the UK

€8.00 in France